LOVE

For Margaret,
a very special friend.

Best wishes,
Iva Nell Elder
Feb. 2, 1984

Gentle Giants

WOMEN WRITERS IN TEXAS

Iva Nell Elder

EAKIN PRESS   AUSTIN, TEXAS

You must do the thing you think you cannot do.

Eleanor Roosevelt
You Learn by Living

To my husband, Joe,
who has always been a source of inspiration
and help to me — with love.

TABLE OF CONTENTS

ABOUT THE AUTHOR

Iva Nell Elder is a native Texan, born in Huntington and raised in Lufkin, in the heart of the East Texas piney woods. She now lives in Houston with her husband and two children.

Her versatility as a writer is apparent as you read her stories and articles. She writes aptly about a cat who made a bird's next his home, *A Home Is Always A Home,* to a more serious article for writers on, *How To Cut Your Manuscript.*

Her formula for selling her writing has been shared many times, as Mrs. Elder speaks to writer's groups, at writer's conferences and seminars.

She is frequently asked to judge short stories and articles for writer's contests and has been highly praised for her in-depth written critique given on each entry. She always takes special interest in the new writer.

Mrs. Elder feels that her experience writing and publishing in the magazine field has helped her in writing her books. She has written more than two hundred short stories, articles and newspaper features. Her articles and stories have appeared in such magazines as *Story World, The Friend, Fun for Middlers, Guide, Counselor, Scripture Press, Scholastic, Young Miss, Venture, Baby Talk, Mother's Manual, Animals, Home Life, Christian Woman, Gospel Herald, Healthways, Child Evangelism* and the 1975 *Writer's Yearbook.*

She has written countless community service articles and feature stories for newspapers.

Her puppet plays and one-act play, *The Gift of Friendship,* have been produced at several churches in the Houston area.

Some of her poems have appeared in church bulletins and have been used in devotional material at various churches.

Her love for writing is apparent as she participates in programs such as a panel sponsored by Houston Community College and aired on KUHT television in Houston, promoting creative writing. She was workshop speaker at the first annual Bluebonnet Festival held at Sam Houston State University in 1983; and featured speaker at the South Plains Writers conference at Texas Tech University in 1983.

She has also been featured speaker at several seminars sponsored by the Associated Authors of Children's Literature, Houston. She has spoken at the National Writers Fiesta in San Antonio, the writing workshop, at Alvin Community College and for the Abilene Writers Conference at Hardin Simmons University.

As a member of the Houston Writers Workshop, Mrs. Elder, along that the other members, sponsored the Southwest Writers' Conference at the University of Houston.

Mrs. Elder felt the need for awards at the conference and named and sponsored the Golden Pen Award for several years until the program could be self sustaining.

Mrs. Elder is a charter member of the Associated Authors of Children's Literature, Houston, and a member of the Houston Writers Workshop. She is a charter member and past president of the Pasadena Writer's Club, and co-founder of the Northshore Writer's Club, Houston.

She is a charter member of the EnAmie Book Review Club where she served as Publicity Chairman and Board Member. She is a member of the Houston Baptist University Auxiliary and a member of the Second Baptist Church, Houston, Texas.

PREFACE

On display in the small, simple boyhood home of Lyndon Baines Johnson, in Johnson City, Texas, is a collection of magazines neatly arranged on a low table. The guide points to these magazines and informs the visitors that Mrs. Johnson, the President's mother, was a writer and had stories published in magazines such as these.

In our vast state of Texas there are many women who are fulfilling their goals as professional writers while maintaining a home, helping their husbands in business or balancing a career of their own. Occasionally they are raising a President.

Most of these women have chosen to stay on the homefront instead of flying the coop and heading for New York or Hollywood to seek their fame and fortune. They have been instrumental in shaping the lives of their family and influencing changes in their own communities with their imaginative ideas and progressive thinking.

Women writers in Texas have good old "Texas grit." At times their writing must fade into the background, until the babies are older or until the "haying is in," but their desire to write never fades completely. It just simmers, like a good savory stew, with time and the right ingredients it bubbles and boils and fills the most discerning appetite.

These gentle giants are determined, energetic women who teach in their local churches, participate in career day and book fairs at their local schools. They take minutes for civic groups, attend conventions with their husbands and work to restore and maintain historical sites in their city and state.

These writers are sprinkled all over the State of Texas. They live and work in the big country, where earth and sky seem to touch. You will find them pounding out exciting short stories in sleepy little towns where life is slow paced and easy.

Many inspirational books are written in rural communities where the whine of a hay bailer or tractor permeates the stillness. Bits of humor are conceived while sitting in an overstuffed chair in a high rise condo. Some writers live in neat houses with well trimmed lawns. But you can be sure that wherever they are, these gentle giants, they add spice and flavor to life. They add color and excitement. These women are not afraid to meet challenges and they face the future with a bright hope and with an unfailing spirit.

These writers come in all sizes and shapes. They are old and young. But their dreams and goals are similar. They have a great determination to succeed and they do — over and over again.

They give us inspirational books like Phyllis Prokop's *How To Wake Up Singing,* Broadman Press.

Pauline Watson's unique style of combining recipes and song, *Cricket's Cookery,* Random House, helps children learn to cook while giving expression to singing. This adds up to a big helping of fun.

Women in Texas are turning out great epic novels, how-to articles, non-sense humor. They write cookbooks, poems and songs. Many impressive children's books are written by these women.

The spotlight is ready and aimed at some of the ''gentle giants'' in Texas, who make us cry, laugh, sing and rejoice with their writings. They challenge us to pick up the pieces after tragedy, they teach us how to manage our money and give us helpful tips on raising our children.

What makes them write? How do they get their ideas and keep producing year after year?

These women will share openly, unashamedly, giving insights into their lives, relating to you their hopes and dreams for the future.

I.N.E.

1

Etta Lynch

"Even with all that's happened in my life I still have to empty the garbage."

There is an extraordinary power at work in each of our lives that helps us fight the battle of self-preservation. Even as a small child we recognize this power and are given certain instincts which enable us to combat some of the hurt and pain in our life. When we follow these instincts we uncap some of our built-up frustrations and have renewed strength to be able to cope with "our present world."

As a small child of nine, Etta Lewis, found a way to alleviate some of the pain and hurt in her life. "I was one of seven children, born during The Great Depression. Life was so grim and money so scarce my father became an alcoholic, then went into drugs. When family crises arose, I wrote out my heartaches, usually when I should have been paying attention in class."

This was her way to self-preservation. Her teacher warned her repeatedly that she must pay attention and not write "notes" in class or she would expose her by reading them aloud. Etta tried to pay attention, but her need to relieve some of the frustrations of the day were so great that she was unable to hold them in. When the teacher made good her threat and snatched a note from Etta's desk, the small frightened girl, grabbed her books, giving no thought to the consequence, and ran from the room. She could not face her fellow students or her teacher. The door did not close fast enough and Etta heard the blatant voice of the teacher reading the note.

Etta Lynch

Today my best friend told me she couldn't be friends with me anymore. Her mother said that my daddy had spent the night in jail. I guess it's true, since he wasn't asleep beside the road this morning like he usually is.

Etta had mixed feelings of resentment and anger. She wanted to get as far away from the classroom as possible, but before she got very far she heard the teacher calling her.

"Etta, wait! Please wait!"

When the teacher caught up with her she threw her arms around Etta's neck holding her close.

"I'm sorry," she whispered. "I'm so sorry. I didn't know."

Etta was stunned by this reaction. "I experienced a sense of separateness, as if I were a third person standing apart and watching. From the first day of school, this teacher had hated me and singled me out for ridicule and humiliation. But after she read those few words scribbled on a piece of paper, her whole attitude had changed. Suddenly she was my friend and ally."

That day as a small child of nine, Etta Lewis, realized the "power of words."

She was to use this *power* time and time again. In the beginning she wrote to relieve her own heartaches, but as time passed she found a new direction for her talent and ability by writing letters for other people.

"I wrote hundreds of letters. Almost always, they were written to mend broken relationships. I wrote a letter a week for a mother whose son was in prison. The mother copied the letters in her own handwriting before sending them to her son. His first reply was my reward and payment."

'Mother, when I read your letter, it was the first time in my life that I thought you really loved me.'

Etta had been given "a gift of writing" and she used the gift to help others.

By the time Etta was eighteen she had been married and divorced and left with two small children to support.

"I enrolled at the Alamo Beauty College in San Antonio. I had to find a way to support myself and my children."

After she finished the course she went home to Abilene for a visit with her family. While there she discovered that her father's alcoholism had worsened. "He rarely worked and when he did he spent his wages on liquor and drugs. I moved back home and began supporting the family. This meant putting five children, including my two, through school.

"I don't regret one minute of it. My sister is a writer. One of my brothers is a medical doctor. Two are heads of departments at Dow Chemical. Both my son and daughter are lawyers. The struggle was worth it."

When her children were teen-agers she moved to Lubbock and married the sweetheart of her childhood, Jimmy Lynch.

"For the first time in my life, I was totally happy."

Five short years later her happiness was shattered by the news that her husband, Jimmy, had cancer. "Six doctors told me he couldn't possibly live longer than two years, and one gave him only six months."

When all of her troubles seemed to be in the past, here she was again faced with yet another heartache, one which threatened her more than any of the rest. But trouble was not an unfamiliar guest in Etta's house. Her courage and faith helped her weather this new turbulent storm in her life.

"When we learned of Jimmy's illness we were devastated. I never prayed harder in my life. I asked everyone I knew to pray for us."

Little did Etta know at that time, that this tragic news, of her husband's illness, was to set her back on her chartered course, and would plunge her into a new and rewarding venture in her life.

"The doctors said I would have to stay home and care for my husband. They urged me to find something that would give me an outlet."

Many things had happened in Etta's life since she was a small girl of nine, sitting in a classroom scribbling her heartaches onto a piece of paper. Life had not always been kind to her, but through all of her trials and troubles, she had never lost the desire to become a writer.

To help fill the void in her life, and to keep her mind busy, Etta enrolled in the Famous Writer's School, a correspondence course, which she could complete at home while caring for her husband. This was to be the stepping stone which would lead her into a long, successful career as a professional writer.

She began to use her "gift for writing" to wash away yet another heartache.

She wrote an article about one of her customers who adopted five brothers between the ages of three and seven. She sent it to Guideposts Magazine.

"I was in the beauty shop when the letter came telling me they wanted the article. I shed tears of gratitude."

This article was published in the April 1966 issue of Guideposts and later, it was syndicated for Lenten Guideposts, which meant a second check for her.

Her lifetime ambition of becoming a writer was finally taking shape. Things began to change in her personal life as well. "An unexplainable medical reversal" occurred and her husband's condition improved. He is still living some eighteen years later.

"It was the answer to the many prayers that were offered in his behalf."

By this time Etta was well on her way to reaching many of the goals she had set for herself as a writer.

At the first writer's workshop she attended she met Helen Reagan Smith, who was teaching creative writing at the University of Oklahoma and conducting workshops.

"This teacher had a tremendous influence in my life. I signed up for the OU correspondence course in professional writing."

After writing several confession stories as a result of her training at OU, she sold one for $375.

"I wrote 16 confession stories and sold 9 of them. Then I was ready to go to some other type of writing."

She began writing "literary" stories and while attending a seminar at Eastern New Mexico University, she entered, *Flee Every Shadow* in the competition. She won the Shamrock Fiction award for that year, 1966.

Her story, *Seed Of Conviction,* won her a prize at the University of Oklahoma competition in 1967.

Etta has written and published more than one hundred-fifty short stories and articles.

They were published in Good Housekeeping, Ladies' Home Journal, Reader's Digest, Home Life and many others.

Her expertise in writing spilled over and she became fiction editor of Teenage Christian and Christian Woman in 1968 and 1969.

Another person to play an important role in Etta's life as a writer was John Allen, editor for Reader's Digest Magazine.

"I met John Allen at a writer's conference and he suggested that I write Jimmy's story, overcoming cancer, plus nine other stories of people overcoming handicaps, and put them into book form."

Help Is Only A Prayer Away, was the result of that conversation. The book was published by Fleming H. Revell Company in 1972.

Two of her other books, *Tender Tyrant: The Legend Of Pete Crawthon:* and *The Tactless Texan* (a biography of Gene Howe) were both written on assignment from Staked Plains Press.

The Power Behind The Comb, was published by Moore Publishing in 1970.

"Almost without exception, the things I write deal with the indomitability of the human spirit. I have a premise that rules my life, and it comes through in my writing, even when I don't intend it. I'm convinced that everyone has a premise, if they'll think about it. Mine is this: There is no handicap so crippling, no obstacle so great, but with faith, prayer, and determination, it can be overcome."

One of her stories, *Davey Swifthands,* has been made into an educational movie, *A Different Drum,* produced by Brigham Young University. This was the first all-Indian movie ever made. The movie garnered the 1975 Cindy Blue Ribbon award, given by the Information Film Producers of America.

Etta is a popular speaker and has lectured at Texas Tech University and conducted workshops for writers at West Texas State University, Hardin Simmons University, Wayland College, and many others.

While her husband was recovering from his illness their big Collie dog, Tuffy, helped him pass the long days with his playful moods and devotion. When Jimmy recovered, the dog died, as if his work was done. Etta was so touched by this friendship between her husband and the dog that she wrote about it, and submitted it to Reader's Digest Magazine. Two weeks later she received a call from Elaine Franklin of Reader's Digest.

"We love your story. We're all in tears over it. But we need one more paragraph."

Within a few days, a check for $2,400 arrived. "This was the largest check I had ever received for a single article."

When her husband retired from his job, at the railroad, Etta was worried. She told him she was proud of him, but she didn't want to retire from her long awaited career as a professional writer and workshop speaker.

"Jimmy told me I didn't have to retire, but could we at least sleep late each morning?"

Etta's day usually begins around ten. "My work day usually begins around noon and I work through the afternoon until four or five."

Etta is still using her talent, as she always has, to help others. Anytime one of her friends or students send up a flare, Etta is willing to give them a helping hand.

Her life is a living example that she believes and lives her own "premise" that there is no obstacle so great, but with faith, prayer and determination it can be overcome. Etta was able to turn to her advantage some of the heartaches of her life, and learn from them and gain strength and develop new interests because of them.

Through all of this she has come away with an irrepressible sense of humor and has learned to accept life, with all of it's challenges, without question.

When a local TV interview with Etta was aired in her hometown, she began to receive many telephone calls from friends lavishing compliments on her. After several calls she grew tired of the same old stock answer of "thank you, you're very kind." Her grand sense of humor surfaced and she told one caller.

"Even with all that's happened in my life I still have to empty the garbage.

"This keeps my head out of the clouds and pulls me out of the writer's trance to face the everyday tasks of keeping a household running and being a wife."

Pauline Watson

2

Pauline Watson

"If you keep your perspective and remember that you are writing to spread joy, there is a good chance that some of your writing will live long enough to give a good many people pleasure."

One day Pauline Watson was busy doing research for one of her articles, when her young son came in with a stream of his friends trailing behind him. When Pauline turned to face her son, he let out a howl.

"Mother, what are you doing?" he rushed his friends back outside. "Why do you have to embarrass me like this? What have you got on your nose?" he demanded.

"Oh, that! It's just a pinto bean."

Pauline was writing an article about all of the things a young child can do with a pinto bean to entertain himself.

Select two toes, place bean between,
you can run a mile on bean gasoline.
If you need a brown wart to wear Halloween,
tape bean to nose top and you will look mean.

"When you write nonsense you have to get rid of your inhibitions. If you want to share with a child through your writing you must be able to cut through the barriers and see the world the way a child does."

Pauline thinks that writing nonsense is a lot like taking up belly dancing. "You've got to be willing to do it regardless of what your friends or family think. And you've got to do it with seriousness and dedication no matter how absurd the idea that has come to you begging to be born into print."

As her children grew and her writing began to become popular, their attitude toward their mother's research changed.

After she had written and published a cookbook for children, *Cricket's Cookery,* combining favorite songs with recipes, to help a child remember the ingredients and make cooking fun for them, she had a call from one of her daughters who was attending A & M University.

"Mother, hold on a minute. I have a surprise for you."

As Pauline pressed the receiver to her ear she heard a chorus of girl's singing one of her recipes, Oh, My Darling Sugar Cookies, to the tune of Oh, My Darling Clementine.

Mash the butter with the sugar;
Stir it twenty-times and then
add the flour, baking powder;
add the salt and stir again.

"This really thrilled my heart. My children were finally beginning to understand that some of the "crazy" research I had to do in order to write for children was worthwhile."

When Pauline was a young girl, living in New Iberia, Louisiana, and attending school, she did a lot of writing for church groups and the Brownie Troops.

"It was something that needed to be done, and I was the one who seemed to know how to do it, so I just did it."

Once she was writing a story for Halloween and it was turning out to be so scary that one of her sisters had to stay up with her so she could finish it.

"I wrote things like, *Bleeding Dell* and *Princess Of The Moon.*"

After finishing high school, she went to work for a Chevrolet Dealership as a bookkeeper. She was still dabbling with her writing. Her best friend worked next door at a china shop, owned by a retired Army Colonel. One day when Pauline was in the shop visiting her friend, Colonel King, knowing her interest in writing, gave her a copy of the Writer magazine.

"This was my first encounter with this publication. I

couldn't believe all the good things in that magazine. I read it from cover to cover.''

Some of the mystery of the publishing world began to unravel for her, and she discovered to her amazement and delight that there were editors, who wanted to buy and publish material like she had been writing.

''People actually got paid for those jokes and anecdotes.''

When she mustered enough courage she sent off a few of her things just for a test. ''When my work began to sell I was thrilled, but I didn't call myself a writer. I didn't even know a writer. There was one writer in our town, but I had never met him, and would never have compared my work to his. Even after I began selling a few fillers and anecdotes I didn't work at my writing. Months would go by before I even thought about submitting anything, then the bug would bite again and off something would go.''

After Pauline married she moved to Texas, living first in Beaumont and finally settled in Houston. Her writing continued this roller coaster pace for several years. When she was twenty-four and pregnant with her first child, her desire to write, and to write well, was beginning to take a prominent place in her life.

''Since I was only working a half day, this seemed to be the ideal time to take a writing course. Once the children started coming, I felt I may not have the opportunity again.''

After some research, she signed up for a home study course offered by The Palmer Institute of Authorship. Because of her involvement with the institute a new and exciting world began to open up for her. She was beginning to fulfill a dream which had been buried so deep inside of her that it had taken her years to even realize it was there.

She began to sell stories to the pulp magazines and sold an anecdote to Reader's Digest.

''I didn't know at that time that Reader's Digest was a hard-to-hit market. I found that out years later.''

But as the years rolled by, Pauline's life was centered more and more around her family. ''My husband and children always had to come first.''

As she tended to the needs of her husband and five children, she began entering contests, which were popular for many years.

"Contesting taught me to write tightly. I wouldn't trade that experience for anything."

Through her contesting she won a pound of bacon for writing the reason she used a certain brand of bacon. For one line, I Never Want My Nickel Back, completing a jingle, Why I Like Coke? she won a T.V. set. It took her three days to think up a winning name for a Shetland pony, but she came up with, L'll Lord Funtoride, and won a pony.

She won a foreign convertible, a treasure hunt on Andros Island and a nine day trip to the West Indies.

"I've had fun with my contesting and was especially thrilled when I won my husband's weight in groceries in a recipe contest. We let the children pick out special items. Mike, our youngest, stocked up on all kinds of cereal, which I'd never allow him to buy when I was watching my purchases. Vicki put twelve pizzas in the cart and Duke, our third son, walked around with nothing but a can of Irish barbecue. But the best part was when we got home and some of the children's friends came over to see our purchases. Their eyes almost popped out when they saw the kitchen table covered with all that junk food."

At one time Pauline had three children in three different schools. From this hectic period in her life, juggling school activities and car pools, she produced two very successful newsaper columns, *Washboard Wisdom* and *Kitchen Klatter,* for Features Unlimited.

Washboard Wisdom, were proverbs set to rhyme:

> Like raindrops
> that mix themselves
> with the seas,
> if you sleep with
> the dogs
> you'll get up
> with the fleas.

Her column, *Kitchen Klatter,* was described as a highly enjoyable, readable and sometimes useful chatter from a housewife.

Pauline believes that writing nonsense can lead a writer to the unexpected. When writing her recipe book for children, *Cricket's Cookery*, Random House, she borrowed the melodies of old songs and fit the instructions into that pattern. She wrote those instructions with so much enthusiasm that when she completed a singing recipe, she found herself singing it over and over just for the fun of it.

When her children were little Pauline kept a notebook in the kitchen and wrote down their bright sayings. She recorded bits of "misunderstood" phrases that children will invariable make. That notebook became a family favorite.

"There is always fresh laughter when a family member flips through the book and sees phrases like— 'and delivery us from weevils, Amen.'

"If you keep your perspective and remember that you are writing to spread joy and not to create great works of art, that will live forever, there is a good chance that some of your nonsense will live long enough to give a good many people pleasure."

But not all of Pauline's work has been in the field of nonsense writing and contesting. The year her oldest daughter graduated from high school, she wrote a story set in the year two-thousand. She tucked it away in the bottom of a drawer and didn't find it again for several years. After she rediscovered the story, she dusted it off, retyped it and entered it in a contest sponsored by the Writer's Digest magazine.

"After that story won the contest, I felt like a writer. Every time I sold something I thought I was a writer — then when I wasn't selling and wasn't even trying to sell I felt like a housewife.

"Once in the middle of the night I had this marvelous idea for a story, so I slipped out of bed and took my pad and pencil into the bathroom and sat there scribbling away. An hour or so later I heard this tap on the door. It was my husband, 'come to sleep, Hemingway,' he prodded. Jimmy didn't mind my scribblings and playing with my writing during the day when he wasn't home, but he needed his breakfast on time the next morning and didn't want me oversleeping. When he was home he expected my attention.''

The story Pauline was working on that night sold to True Story for $250. ''We paid for part of a fence from that sale. This gave me so much encouragement. I could look out back and see the fence and know that my writing had helped pay for it.''

As soon as the story sold, she started working on another one for the same magazine. The editor liked the story and asked her to change the ending, but since this was a true story, she didn't feel she should tamper with the ending and tucked it away in a drawer. A couple of years went by before she decided to heed the editor's advice and change the ending. She retyped the story, sent it off and it sold.

The turning point in Pauline's attitude toward her writing came after she won the Writer's Digest contest. A representative of the Houston Writer's Workshop, Johnny Bass, called her and invited her to come to a meeting. Pauline refused. She did not think she was qualified to become involved with a group of professional writers.

''Johnny didn't give up. She called a second time. She told me that the group met informally and just talked writing. She convinced me that I was well qualified to attend. Even though my family always had to come first, I knew I wanted some type of involvement with other writers, so I consented to go. After that meeting I was really charged up. From that point on I made a vow to myself that I would never again say 'I'm trying to write,' I was going to be more positive. ''Trying'' had to go. I *was* writing and I *would always write.''*

Many friendships grew out of that group. One very important influence in Pauline's life was Ellen Goins, an illustrator-writer.

''Ellen had a way of seeing worth in a person. She could look into someone's longings and just by her encouragement could bring them up to their very best. She told me once that the reason I had never felt like a writer was because all of my stuff was scattered everywhere. Tucked away in that secure drawer. She encouraged me to get it out and put it all together.''

Because of Pauline's association with this group of writers her ideas, attitudes and aspirations changed.

"I learned that these people were just like me, with one difference. They believed and confirmed that they were professional writers."

The encouragement she received from this group brought her out of the world of being a part-time writer and into the world of the professional writer. Her attitude toward her writing was changing.

"Once when I was about twenty I won a contest writing about My Favorite Neighbor. The article was read over the radio. My neighbor received an orchid from the sponsoring flower shop and I received a gold tipped vase. When I went to pick up my prize, the lady at the shop looked at me and said, 'you have really missed your calling. You should have been a writer.' and I said "yeah!" Since I was already twenty and working as a bookkeeper, it was just too bad, even though I had a deep inner longing to write, I had missed "my calling."

Reflecting back on those memories, Pauline shutters and laughs. "So many things have changed since then. I have learned so much. Emerson said it so well, 'people are what they think all day long. Your life is what your thoughts make of it.' Since I thought I was a bookkeeper — I was a bookkeeper. William James says, 'the human being, by changing the inner attitude of the mind, can change the outer aspect of their lives.'

New revelations were unfolding for Pauline. She was beginning to heed some of the advice she had gleaned from these two famous men. After attending several meetings of the Houston Writer's Workshop, she began to change her thinking pattern. She was no longer going to think of herself as just a wife and mother. She was also a writer. From that time on she began to think like a writer, work like a writer and therefore she was becoming a professional writer. For better or worse, she knew this was "her calling" and she intended to use what talent she had to spread joy for others.

Soon after this Pauline's work began to sell regularly. Her articles, stories, fillers and anecdotes have appeared in Reader's Digest, Woman's Day, Southern Living, Parent's Magazine,

Tempo, Cricket, My Weekly Reader and many others.

In 1971 Pauline became interested in writing books for children and was a charter member of the Associated Authors of Children's Literature, Houston, an offshoot of the Houston Writer's Workshop. She believes that writing for children is the "highest form of writing. It has to be pure."

Once when Pauline left out an ingredient in one of her singing recipes, published in Cricket Magazine, several readers quickly called her attention to the mistake.

"In typing my final draft for the recipe, Merry Cornbread Cake, I left out a key ingredient, milk. Several young readers tried the recipe and discovered, as one little girl put it, that the recipe didn't work. 'It was just a big glob.' I felt terrible about the mistake. I sent a personal letter of apology along with a corrected copy of the recipe to each of the readers who had written. One little girl wrote back and said she was thrilled about the mistake, because she had enjoyed the personal letter and new recipe. She was going to take the letter to school with her to share with her firends. Another reader wrote and told me that she wasn't mad at me. She sent me her report card, so I guess she did forgive me for that mistake."

Pauline's first children's book was published in 1974. She has had one published almost every year since then. *A Surprise For Mother,* Prentice Hall, 1976, *Curley Cat Babysits,* Harcourt, Brace, Jovanovich, 1977, *Days With Daddy,* Prentice Hall, 1977, *Cricket's Cookery,* Random House, 1977, *Wriggles, The Little Wishing Pig,* The Seabury Press, 1978, *What Would You Do?* Prentice Hall, 1979, *The Walking Coat,* Walker and Company, 1980; and *My Turn, Your Turn,* Prentice Hall.

All of Pauline's children are grown now, but she still maintains contact with children and is still doing research for her stories, which she feels is vitally important when writing for this age group.

She takes six books out of the library, then invites a five-year old neighbor in for lunch. She lets the child choose one of the books to read. This keeps her in touch with what children enjoy in books.

"Writing has become a very important part of my life. As

long as I'm able to be excited about the venture I think I will always write. I feel that if you are excited about what you are doing, you'll create an aura of good cheer that will surround your work—a feeling that will project itself to your reader. When you are writing for children you have to not mind laughing at yourself and with the child. If you can't do this it will be hard to relate to a child reader. I could never have written my singing recipes if I had not followed this philosophy. I may not have ever written:

> Oh my darling, oh my darling,
> Sugar cookies, you are fun!
> You will soon be in the oven
> In my tummy when you're done.

"Early in my life I didn't know that I would someday be a writer. But there were signs all along the way. When I was very young, I would write poems and songs and sing them to the big pecan tree in my back yard. I *know* that tree listened.

"To the aspiring writers of today I would just say, bring a naturalness and a kindness into your writing. Spread joy and don't be afraid to be identified with the professional. You are what you think you are all day long."

Marilyn Cooley

3

Marilyn Cooley

"I have always thrived on deadlines and competition."

As a fifth grade student, attending Shields Heights elementary school in Oklahoma City, Marilyn Cooley was very much aware of her desire to write. Her first venture into the writing field was a one page newspaper, written and distributed to her classmates. The newspaper contained many timely articles and bits of up to the minute reporting.

"I wrote things like, Hattie Sue wore a new pink dress to school Monday."

From this early age Marilyn's big desire and goal was to one day work as a foreign correspondent. But this goal was shattered in her junior year of college when she met and married, Ray Cooley. "By this time writing was a big part of my life and I knew I would always write, but the foreign was reduced to local because I didn't want to be apart from my husband."

While pursuing a journalism degree from the University of Oklahoma, Marilyn, worked on the university newspaper, *The Oklahoma Daily*. Her first by-line came by accident when she was a sophomore. "My regular beat was reporting on the Drama School activities. It was a slow time, not much going on, so I just wrote what I thought was an interesting story and turned it in."

The story was published in the paper the next day and carried a by-line. "I was so impressed and very surprised. They told me it was a very good feature article and they were pleased with the way it had turned out. I didn't even know it was a feature article. In those days I did things without really knowing what I was doing and people liked it.''

That same year, Marilyn, was named Outstanding Sophomore Woman of the Year in the journalism school.

By the time she was a senior she was pregnant, but she did not let this detour her from pursuing her career goals. That same year she became editor of the paper and loved every minute of it.

"We would put the paper to bed every night around ten or eleven, five days a week. It was work, but very rewarding.''

There were many valuable lessons Marilyn learned while working on the paper. One of her Professors stressed the advantages of being prepared when conducting interviews. He told his students to arm themselves with lots of notes and be prepared for the unexpected. Marilyn intended to follow the Professor's suggestions, but since interviews had always come so easy and naturally for her she usually armed herself with only a few pertinent facts, leaving the rest to her natural ability and to luck. Most of the time she just went in cold, introduced herself, talked a bit, and came away with enough material for her article.

One day she was scheduled to interview one of the Law Professors, and went in, sat across from him at his desk, as confident as always, but not as prepared as she should have been, and found to her surprise that the Law Professor was very hostile. This was the first time she had ever been confronted with "yes" and "no" answers.

"Someone had done an article on this Professor before for the paper and he didn't like the way it had turned out. He wasn't about to be caught off guard again. All he intended to do was answer my questions, and since I wasn't prepared with a list of questions the interview was a disaster. After that I learned the value of preparation.''

After graduating from the University of Oklahoma with a BA in journalism, Marilyn continued her career in the newspaper business. She worked for The United Press, and later edited a bi-weekly newspaper, *The Capitol Hill Beacon.* "I always seemed to thrive on deadlines and competition.'' In the course of her career she also edited a monthly in-house magazine, *Commerce and Industry.*

After she moved to Texas and settled in Houston, she worked with her husband in the advertising business. "I worked in the production department and hated it, but it was good for me because I learned to handle details."

When the business was established she decided it was time for her to stay home and spend more time with her young daughter, K. C. "In those years while I was home with K. C., I wrote when I could (mostly unproductively) and worked outside the home when we were in desperate straits."

It was during this time that she learned that confession magazines paid well. "I decided to try my hand at writing fiction."

Even though she sold confession stories she never felt comfortable with this type of writing.

"Confessions have to be written using a strict format. I knew the formula, but it was hard for me to write to their specifications."

She vividly recalls the last confession story she wrote and sold. At that time she was handling the family budget, mostly juggling the money, desperately trying to make it stretch to cover all of the bills. Her lack of expertise in handling the money caught up with her and the inevitable happened and she found herself in deep money difficulties.

"I was overdrawn at the bank and needed money badly, but I couldn't bring myself to tell my husband. The only way I knew to earn some quick money was by writing a confession story. I sat down and wrote a story about a girl who was living in the city with another girl and she was having money problems. I felt like an expert on this subject. The girl's friend is going out with some out of town business men and wants the girl to go with her. She doesn't approve, the men are probably married, but she's hungry and desperate so she goes. One thing leads to another and she finds herself going to a party with one of the men. A couple of lines in the story went something like, 'he came on like a bear. She needed a whip and chair to protect herself.' Of course, the girl's virtue remained intact, which was a must in those days and she got out of a bad situation after learning from the experience.

"It was September and I just knew the story would sell

quickly, but it didn't sell quick enough to pull me out of my money troubles then, but it did sell before Christmas. By then I was in another hole and the money came in handy.''

Her career was to take on another dimension in 1977 when she met Dr. Mary Elizabeth Schlayer, who was conducting seminars across the United States for women on finance.

Marilyn was having lunch with her friend, Raelle Frost, who worked with Dr. Schlayer in the seminars.

''Raelle started telling me about the seminars. I wasn't that interested at first, but the more she talked the more interested I became. Not from the standpoint of gaining knowledge, but my writing nose could sniff out a good story and I saw the possibility of an article.''

They arranged a luncheon meeting with Dr. Schlayer at Raelle's home. After lunch when Marilyn and Dr. Schlayer began discussing the possibility of an article, Marilyn learned that Dr. Schlayer was already anticipating writing a book with another writer.

''When I learned about the book, I dropped the article idea. Frankly, I was relieved. Being a lazy writer I could already see that there would be a lot of work involved. On my way home I went by the store and bought some paint. Since I wasn't going to do the article I would just paint.''

About a month later Raelle called and told Marilyn that the woman who was going to collaborate with Dr. Schlayer on the Money book had backed out. She wanted to know if Marilyn would be interested. It didn't take her long to make a decision. ''I couldn't resist the challenge.''

''Since Dr. Schlayer was the money expert, she was to do the research and I was to write the book. It didn't work out just as we had planned. I did have to pitch in and do a lot more than our original bargain. When you are co-authoring a book it's good to lay your ground rules first and approach your writing in a business like manner so that everyone knows where they stand. We had a firm contract between us before we began the project.''

Marilyn wrote thirty pages on life insurance, put it with a one page outline, and sent it off. The book proposal sold within a week and a half. She attributes the fast sale and the success of the book to the subject matter. Women and their finances. Thus, *How To Be A Financially Secure Woman,* was born.

Rawson Associates Publishers, Inc., bought the book and gave them a six months deadline. They thought they had a free hand concerning the format and proceeded with the writing.

"I worked mostly from tapes. Dr. Schlayer provided the expertise and I did the writing."

The book sold in August and was to be finished by January 31. Everything was going smoothly until the middle of December when Marilyn received a letter from Eleanor Rawson, their editor. She didn't like the format they were using.

"She didn't want the book rewritten, but rearranged. She also wanted some additional chapters, dealing with the single woman and how the young woman could get ahead in her career. So I did the additional writing and a lot of cutting and pasting. This seemed to please her."

Before the book came out the Literary Guild and The Book Club, Doubleday and Company, were both bidding on the book. Marilyn was in New York City, attending the annual meeting of The Mystery Writer's of America, when she learned the outcome of the bidding.

The first morning of the meeting she was sitting at a big round table playing Clue with Julian Simon from London and several other well known mystery writers, when she received a message that her agent was trying to get in touch with her.

"I felt so conspicuous. Here I was sitting at a table with these famous writers and I was worried because I thought they might think that this little upstart had arranged for that message to be delivered to the table to call attention to herself. I was so uncomfortable. After the game was over I rushed out and called my agent."

The good news was that the book had sold to Literary Guild and it had sold for sixty-five thousand dollars.

"I was thrilled. I remember walking in Times Square and thinking that I had "peaked." Everything from this point on would be downhill. That was a sad thought on such a happy day."

Bantam bought the paperback rights and it was excerpted

in Cosmopolitan and Today's Woman magazines. It is still active in the market place. Sales are brisk. The New Woman magazine had excerpts from the book in the June 1981 issue. It is now the official textbook for Dr. Schlayer's seminars.

Recently it was used when Dr. Schlayer gave a six weeks seminar for PBS television, originating from channel 8 in Houston.

Marilyn's next book, *Checklist For A Working Wife,* was written on assignment for Doubleday, for their Dolphine division.

"Lindy Hess was my editor on this book. Doubleday had done a couple of checklist books before. One on weddings and one on entertaining. The checklist for working wives was to be 120 pages and they gave me a six months deadline.

"I enjoyed writing the book, but since I had never been a very organized person, I had to sit down and figure out how to organize yourself for maximum time and energy when you are working."

When Marilyn is working on deadline her day begins around nine. She works until noon, takes a break, and is back at her desk from two until five.

"When I'm not on deadline, I don't work that much. I find that I get very restless writing non-fiction. I have to get up and walk around more. I don't get as restless when I'm writing fiction. In fiction you're in the story, living the experiences along with the characters. You get caught up in their lives and lose yourself for awhile. As a general rule, I think non-fiction pays better than fiction unless you have a big block buster. You handle non-fiction very much like fiction. You try to create an interesting story. The technique is similar."

In the past few years, the mystery novel, has become Marilyn's first love. "I haven't sold a mystery novel yet, but a publisher was seriously considering one of mine and held it for a year, but they switched their emphasis from mysteries to romance novels, so they sent it back."

Her favorite mystery writers are Agatha Christie, P. D. James, from England, and William Kienzler, an American.

"William Kienzler is my very favorite mystery writer. He

writes lovely, lovely books. I'm intrigued with them. His main character is a former priest. Mr. Kienzler was a priest for ten years and because of this background his main character really comes alive. The book always deal with good and bad. The gray area. The characters are usually involved in something which isn't legally wrong, but things that harm people. He deals with a real moral situation. Mr. Kienzler is the only author who has ever written me a note after I reviewed his book. It was a thank you note and a real joy to receive."

For the past few years, Marilyn, has been reviewing mysteries for the *Houston Chronicle* newspaper. During this time she has found that there seems to be a decline in the deductive mystery. There is some suspense, but the espionage, the spy books, are making a strong impact on the market.

Marilyn attributes much of her success in writing to a simple and very basic idea. "This idea came to me like a flash of realization. It's one of those things that's so basic that you would think everyone would know it. All my writing career I have been aiming my material toward the editors and publishers. It suddenly occurred to me that if I wrote something that would make them money they would snap it up. They must be profitable to stay in business. This is so basic, but so often overlooked. Aim your material for the public, your reader, it will have a better chance of selling."

To the aspiring writer, Marilyn, stresses the importance of surrounding yourself with a professional aura. One that will project itself both to the editors and to the public.

"It's so important to be professional in your approach to writing. Set aside some time to write and write every day. One of my Professors at the University, Foster Harris, said that people who had only written short pieces were afraid to tackle a book, but it's just like climbing a mountain. Before you can get to the top you must take the first step and continue one step at a time until you reach the top. With writing, you just take one paragraph at a time until you have a page and one page at a time until you finish your book. If you approach your writing this way it will not be so overwhelming."

If Marilyn had been afraid to accept new challenges and be

content where she was in her writing life, she could not have started her climb to the top of the mountain. If she had not grabbed hold of the challenges, reached beyond for new ideas and new ways of approaching her writing goals, someone else would have written the books she wrote, created the characters she created, and reaped the benefits of all of them.

But Marilyn was not afraid to accept the new challenges, and therefore she did write the books, create the characters, and reaped the joys and satisfaction only a writer can feel after a good days work and she has reaped the benefits of knowing that she has taken a blank piece of paper and made things happen in a way no one else could have. The rewards have been many and she has the added pleasure of knowing that there's more money in the bank because of her efforts.

4

Suzanne Morris

"I hope never to be guilty of writing the same story more than once."

In the course of most writer's careers they receive enough rejection slips to paper a bathroom wall. Springboards of conversation are built around them and writers compare their rejection slips as cooks compare their favorite recipes. At the Reader's Digest Writer's Conference held in San Marcos, Texas, a set of long horns and a phonograph record were awarded to the writer who admitted receiving the most rejections.

What is a writer without her fair share of rejection slips? A lucky writer — Perhaps!

Suzanne Morris had only collected two when her blockbusting, historical novel, *Galveston,* hit the marketplace.

"I sent an outline to one publisher before Doubleday bought the book, and they turned it down. When the manuscript was completed I sent it to an agent, who had expressed an interest, but he said he didn't think it was marketable."

In the early summer of 1975, Doubleday bought the book and offered Suzanne a two-book contract. By September they had negotiated paperback reprint rights with Bantam Books, and sold it to the Book Club division of their own company. Even before publication the book was optioned to Universal Pictures and sold to three foreign countries, England, South Amer-

Suzanne Morris

ica and Holland. This brought Suzanne a sizable income in the six figure range.

The book was published in 1976 and won the First Novel Award from critic, Evelyn Oppenheimer. The book was a best seller and became popular internationally.

This work did not come easily or without effort. Many years of training, research and hard work were plowed into the developing and writing of the book.

When Suzanne was a child she wanted to write, but the closest she came to doing anything concrete about it was entertaining her classmates with her mystery stories. As a college student at the University of Houston, she took some journalism courses, but felt that they were not steering her in the right direction.

After she married and moved to Tacoma, Washington, with her husband, who was in the army, she began to explore the possibiliies of taking some college courses.

"Even though I had a full-time job, I still had some time on my hands. I checked with the community college about their creative writing class and they put me in touch with Rega McCarty.

"When I had talked to creative writing teachers before, I had always been somewhat turned off by them. This was my first encounter with a teacher who had an encouraging attitude."

From the beginning, Suzanne learned that this teacher believed in her ability as a writer and because of this, she was able to guide her in the direction of her ultimate goal, of someday writing fiction.

"I had always wanted to write fiction, but I wasn't sure that I could. Rega believed in me more than I believed in myself. If she hadn't been there at that point in my life, I probably wouldn't be writing today. She gave me the training that was so important, plus, of course, plenty of encouragement."

Even though she was an avid reader of fiction and was influenced by the work of Daphne du Maurier, Suzanne had a stigma about writing fiction and was afraid to even try. She had done quite a lot of non-fiction articles with historical backgrounds, but never felt this type of writing was fulfilling.

"For me the only type of creative writing was fiction. It had always been my first love. I really wanted to do it, but up until I met Rega, I never had the courage to tackle a fiction project.

"I think a lot of my problem was that I thought the story had to be fully plotted first and then you added the characters. Then I began to realize that for me, plotting was secondary, and the characters were the real beginning.

"Once I have one or two major characters in mind, I let the

story develop around them, because of who they are and what they feel and do."

Galveston was her first fiction project, as well as her first novel. When the idea for the novel began to grow and develop, Suzanne knew that she must not let the idea simmer too long or she may lose her enthusiasm. But by the time she had mustered enough nerve to tackle a big fiction project, other problems surfaced.

"When I became serious about getting down to writing the book, I gave up a full time job, knowing that I just couldn't do both. I knew that I would need to spend two or three days a week in Galveston doing research. During this time, my husband was starting a second business, and since I had always been involved in his business, keeping the books and other administrative duties, he couldn't understand my timing.

"He came in one day and saw all of the bookkeeping, for both companies, stacked up on my desk and was quite annoyed. He asked, 'don't you think you could put off writing that book for awhile?' I told him 'no.'

"I felt even then that once a story is ready to be written, it's death to put it off."

In the midst of her personal adjustment of trying to soft peddle her involvement in her husband's business and her time consuming schedule of researching the book, she became pregnant.

Her son, Quentin, was born a few weeks after she completed the manuscript, and the work was safely tucked away for several months while she adjusted to her new role as mother.

Even though Suzanne did not come from a literary background, her parents had a profound influence in shaping her life and in a sense helped prepare her for a writing career.

"My father is an artist and therefore a visual person. Since I have been around him all of my life, I too have developed this trait. When I read a book I like to see things. To get a picture in my mind. I don't want to float around, but have my feet rooted in the place and in the time of the story. When I'm writing fiction I try to create pictures.

"My mother always pressed me into trying new things. She

encouraged me in my dancing and music. She wanted me to be involved in all kinds of creative outlets. I have been on stage with my music and dancing most of my life. Perhaps, without knowing it, my mother was preparing me for the promotional end of my writing career, as well as giving me self-confidence.''

After she had adjusted somewhat to her new role as mother, Suzanne again turned her attention to her writing. She attended the Southwest Writer's Conference in Houston and met William Goyen, a well known writer and editor.

She attended his workshops and afterward contacted him and asked if he would look at her manuscript, *Galveston.*

"Bill read the manuscript and liked it very much. At that time Doubleday was his publisher and he brought it to their attention and they bought it.''

When the book came out Suzanne was thrust into a very hectic promotional schedule. She traveled all over Texas, promoting the book and had interviews both in and out of the State. This resulted in additional problems. She was now a mother as well as a wife. Arrangements had to be made for her son's care.

"We had been married eleven years when Quentin was born. We were accustomed to doing things whenever we wanted to. I could write anytime — late at night, all week-end if I chose to — but now, all that changed. With a child you have to maintain some sort of schedule.

"I found that I didn't have time to fit everything into my life that I wanted to, so again I decided that I didn't want to be so active in my husband's business.

"Through the years my level of participation with the company has changed many, many times. If my husband needs me really badly, then that is my number one priority and I do nothing but that for several months. During those times I write very little.''

It was hard for her husband to adjust to a two career family.

"I don't think anyone functions on just one level. A part of my husband said this is wonderful and I'm proud for my wife. He was always proud of anything I did creatively, whether it was dancing or music or writing. He was always very supportive. One part of him said I'm proud, but the other part said, this is getting in my way.''

At a time when she should have been sitting on top of the world, she found her problems snowballing.

''Suddenly I was thrust into a totally new kind of existence. I didn't know what it was like to promote a book. I couldn't believe it. I was traveling all the time. There were speaking engagements, autographing parties, television and newspaper interviews. Doubleday had given me a two book contract and I was serious about getting on with my next book. I was trying to promote one book, write and research another, and tend to my family. It was very difficult.

''My next novel was *Keeping Secrets.* I was somewhat frightened by the success that *Galveston* enjoyed, but I knew I couldn't remain productive and worry about what I had done in the past. I had to put *Galveston* out of my mind and move on. I wanted to produce a good book, and I didn't want to rewrite *Galveston.* I hope never to be guilty of writing the same story twice.''

Keeping Secrets is set in San Antonio, Texas, during the period, 1914-1918. Suzanne made five week-long trips to San Antonio, studying at the San Antonio Conservation Society, The Main Library, the D.R.T. Library, and interviewing a number of people who had either been alive during the story period, or were descendants of people who had lived in San Antonio at that time. She spent about twice the amount of research time on *Keeping Secrets,* as she did on *Galveston* and ironically when *Galveston* was completed it turned out to be 729 pages, with a 40-year story span, while *Keeping Secrets* was 629 pages, with a 4-year story span.

The story involves intrigue and espionage dealing with things that brought America into World War I. The Mexican Revolution was also going on at the same time, and was interconnected. As with *Galveston,* the story came to Suzanne, through the major characters. She wrote the story for them.

Part of Suzanne's research entailed reading the daily *San Antonio Express* newspaper on microfilm covering a period of five years. She read every issue. That alone was a tremendous project. But she finally reached a point when she had to cut off the research and start writing the book.

During this same period they started having some problems with their son, Quentin, who was three. "I don't know if we had problems with him or he had problems with us. This was one of the most difficult times in my life. There was so much tension in our home that I told my husband that if he wanted me to, I would stop writing after I fulfilled my contract with Doubleday and finished *Keeping Secrets.* I was willing to do anything to relieve the stress. He said, 'no, don't stop writing. We'll work out our problems.'

In early 1978, Suzanne was alerted by her son's preschool teacher that he was exhibiting some disturbing behavioral signs. He was withdrawn and unable to relate to the other children. He had uncontrollable fits of temper, and was often afraid for no apparent reason.

His teacher felt that he needed to undergo some psychological testing, and put them in touch with a doctor.

"The results of those tests were inconclusive. The doctor felt Quentin might benefit from therapy, and that my husband and I should devote time to family therapy.

"The doctor confirmed the teacher's observations that Quentin was unable to relate to others in a cognitive manner and cautioned that, while not at that time psychotic, he could become so unless therapy was begun at an early age.

"The doctor made a comment that would stay with me for a long time. At that time I didn't know precisely what he meant. 'Quentin hugged my neck when I was leaving school yesterday. I know from this reaction that he is not autistic.' No one at the school told me that they had suspected Quentin was autistic. I'm not sure what I would have done if I had even suspected this was his problem."

Quentin displayed a lot of symptoms associated with the syndrome. One of his favorite toys was a clear bubble filled with colored balls. He was fascinated with the toy and spent hours spinning it. He carried around a little piece of garden hose instead of a teddy bear and he rocked himself incessantly.

To further document the evidence, parents of a child with

these symptoms were usually above average in intelligence, often creative and involved in career pursuits. Very often the syndrome would appear in a male child, the firstborn.

"After learning the symptoms of an autistic child from a nurse friend, I was very grateful for the comment the doctor had made. Even though Quentin displayed many of the traits of autism, this had been ruled out."

Even so, they were still faced with many decisions concerning their son.

"While I was trying to decide on the best route of therapy for Quentin, I was faced with the added burden of a husband who believed the whole sequence had gone too far already. He thought everyone was making too much of the situation. He refused to be intimidated by what anyone said about his son. He was determined to follow his own instincts. He felt that Quentin needed a change. We took him out of that school and enrolled him in a school closer to home and he began to thrive. We did continue to work with him at home and try to bring him out of his shell and we encouraged him to interact more with other children. We ruled out professional therapy.

"Parents always want what is best for their child and when the experts start talking, you should listen. The teacher's intentions were good; there were no villains. The main problem with Quentin was that we were trying to press social abilities on him which he wasn't ready to accept. For a long time nobody knew how to deal with the fact that his interests were different from those of the other children. There was a lot of worry when there shouldn't have been.

"Since I was so busy, I began to let everyone tell me what to do and I stopped listening to my own God-given instincts. Since I was raising him in such an unusual way, I tended not to have any confidence in what I felt. Quentin is seven now and is very bright, but his interests are still different from other children.

"It's not easy to raise a child. There's a lot of responsibility attached to it. You have so much in your hands. I worry, perhaps a little too much, about the kind of job I'm doing with my son. But the mistakes of several years ago have taught me something. I'm more confident now.''

Some of the experiences and problems Suzanne encountered with her son formed the basis for her novel *Skychild,* published by Doubleday, 1981. She is quick to say that this is not autobiographical.

''In writing *Skychild,* I meant to cast no stones, except possibly at myself and others who allow our basic instincts about our children to be undermined by well-meaning experts and teachers, who know our child in a limited way. We should listen to our own inner voice and use it as a filtering system.

''The book is fiction, but I think it touches on many of the real predicaments which career women find themselves in today. It's not easy to combine marriage and parenting with a career. Even though working mothers have become socially accepted, and are urged to lead self-fulfilling lives, we are still victims of much self-doubt about whether we are fulfilling all the roles expected of us by our husbands and families, while we are trying to reach the goals we set for ourselves.

''When I first started writing this story, my viewpoint character was the mother, Monica Maguire, but after I had completed the first draft. I knew something was wrong. I was disappointed in the lack of vitality in the story. It seemed to plod along unexcitingly. The four-year-old child, Ian, whom I needed most to capture, remained elusive: a stick figure. Then I decided to try something totally different. I got inside Ian and wrote out. I took every symptom he displayed and tried to figure out why he might react the way he did. I began to view the world through his eyes. The story began to come alive.

''If I had told my editor that I was writing 25% of the book from the child's viewpoint, she may have said, 'forget it'. That will never work.'

''But I think that if a writer feels something is right, even though all the books say don't do it that way, do it, because it's probably best.''

In early October 1980, the editor of *In-Between* magazine, published in Galveston, Texas, commissioned Suzanne to write an article about Ashton Villa, one of the historical houses on the island. At that time she was again working full time at her husband's office, and felt this would be a good quick writing assignment and was eager to accept. But she soon realized that there was a great deal of research involved in the project.

"When my book, *Galveston*, came out, I was honored with a big party in Galveston at Ashton Villa. I was impressed with the house, but really knew nothing of the background. When I began my research I couldn't find any new material on the Brown family who had built the mansion. I knew that if I didn't get a fresh handle on the subject, nobody in Galveston would be interested in reading the article. But after I started digging, things opened up, and I heard from some of the descendants of the Browns. A family member in San Francisco sent a lot of good material that I could use."

The article has been reprinted in tabloid form and is sold at the Ashton Villa gift shop.

Suzanne says that writing takes a great deal of discipline.

"Writing is not an easy profession. You have to put a lot of time and effort into it if you really want it to be good. Most of my writing, even though it has been fiction, required a lot of research, but I loved every moment. I don't think I've ever done anything that was as rewarding or as fulfilling.

"My work schedule is different now than it used to be. I usually don't work in the evenings or on weekends. I try to reserve this time for my family.

"We enjoy entertaining friends in our home and occasionally spend an evening out, but since we are a two-career family, we have to arrange our time as well as possible around our son, so we gear much of our free time to activities he enjoys."

Suzanne is involved in another book project and expects to have a fourth book in the marketplace soon.

5

Elizabeth Silverthorne

"I write what I like to write. What I care about. I have never been able to write to any specifications other than my own."

When Elizabeth Silverthorne was writing her book, *The Ghost Of Padre Island,* she held a full time teaching job, was the wife of a busy doctor and the mother of two active teen-agers.

"It took me over a year to write that book because I wrote in scraps and bits of time."

Elizabeth utilized those scraps and bits of time and found that she could write while waiting for her son to finish basket-ball practice, in the dentist's office waiting room or in between social and civic activities.

On Saturday morning she drove her daughter to a small town fifteen miles outside of Temple for her weekly music les-sons. After she dropped her daughter off, she headed for one of her favorite writing spots, a nearby cemetery.

"The cemetery was very peaceful and quiet. I got a lot of writing done there."

From the early age of ten, Elizabeth has had a compulsion to put things into words.

"I had this feeling that things were not really true until I

Elizabeth Silverthorne

had written them down. If I took a trip I had to write about it. An event became real to me only after I had written about it.

When she was a student in elementary school through her high school years, Elizabeth participated in the interscholastic league writing contests. Her interest in writing continued to play an important role in her life and she became editor of the high school newspaper and the school annual. She achieved the high honor of valedictorian of her class.

While she was in college she contributed to the college literary magazines, but did not try to market any other work until after she was married and her children were in high school.

Elizabeth grew up the middle child in a family of six.

"I have four sisters and one brother who was killed in an automobile accident when he was twelve. All of my sisters are still living."

Elizabeth's father was a doctor and her mother was a teacher and a writer.

"I was definitely influenced by the fact that my mother was always writing and collecting material for articles and stories. She had a children's book published when I was very young. This really impressed me. Unfortunately, she didn't know anything about marketing and sold all of her rights so she didn't realize as much financial reward as she should have. One of her stories on rodeos was picked up and put in an anthology."

Her father died when she was a young teen, and her mother took the children and went home to live with her mother in Angleton, Texas.

"My mother was English and her family was lured to Texas as many other English families were by promises of getting rich raising cotton and cattle. Of course, that didn't turn out to be the case usually, but a whole group of English people came and settled in and around Angleton."

Elizabeth has always had an intense desire to travel and this is what led her into accepting a job as stewardess for Pan American World Airways. Because of her travels with the airline she has consciously and unconsciously collected a great deal of material to be used as background information in her writing.

"I have never published anything with a stewardess as protagonist, but I am working on a story now. It's getting a little out of hand as a short story and I think it might turn into a novel."

Elizabeth encountered some very frightening experiences while flying. "Fire in the air poses the most danger. If fire develops in the engine or the electrical system it's usually very serious. There were a few times this happened, but fortunately each time the safety system worked. I have been in some very bad storms and during those times you reexamine your life and wonder, 'what am I doing up here?' You may take a vow that if you ever get down that you will never come back, but you do.''

The airline had a rule against married women working as a stewardess, and since Elizabeth married while working for the airlines she couldn't fly, but when they joined the union this rule was lifted and she became the first married stewardess to fly for Pan American.

''In those days when you served eggs at altitude they sometimes turned green because of a lack of oxygen. I had never been air sick before, but one day I was serving these green eggs and became very ill. When I got back on the ground, I found out I was pregnant. I quit flying after that.''

Elizabeth and her husband Dr. M. Clark Silverthorne settled in Temple, where he carried on his medical practice and she taught at the Temple Junior College.

''Someone named Silverthorne signed the marriage certificate of Robert Browning and Elizabeth Barrett. We have never found out if there's a connection with our family, but we hope so. My husband's father was a Methodist minister so there may have been other ministers down the line.

''Silverthorne is an English name. My husband's father was born in England, but my husband grew up in Scarsdale, a bedroom community of New York City.''

One of Elizabeth's first articles was written as a result of one of her pet peeves. It was *Those Magnificent Monsters*, and was sold to Young World, a children's magazine.

''I have always been interested in mythology and when I discovered that my children were not being taught about the gods and goddesses or the stories behind them, I began to rewrite some of the myths for them. I felt it was important for them to have their mythology as a reference in poetry, art and music. The simple myths should be taught as early as kindergarten and build each year so that the students will be ready to go into more depth when they are in high school.''

Her first article was written because there was a chasm to be filled, but her first short story, came as a result of a deep seated memory.

"One of my sisters was scheduled to be married and had everything arranged. The minister was hired, the flowers ordered and the guests invited. The day before the wedding someone from the county clerk's office called and informed her that if she married on the day she had planned that the wedding would be illegal because her blood test would have expired.

"In those days your blood test had to be twenty-one days before the wedding. This meant she would have to take another blood test and wait another twenty-one days. Everybody panicked. We didn't know what to do. My sister put in a frantic call to the minister and he suggested that the actual wedding ceremony be performed during the rehearsal and the next day the guests could witness the rehearsal, without knowing any of the problems.

"My brother-in-law was rather disgusted with the whole thing and it wouldn't have bothered him to just whisk his new bride away after they were legally married.

"It was all confusing and interesting. Anytime the family got together in after years we always talked about the wedding. I kept thinking that this would make a good story and finally wrote it and sold it to Mature Years magazine. It came out as, *A Bird In Hand,* in the May, 1974 issue.

"This shows something of my career. From Young World to Mature Years. I haven't really settled down into one field. I write what I like to write. What I care about. This is the reason I write for all different ages."

Elizabeth's first book came as a result of attending a writer's conference at Buell College in Denver, Colorado. She submitted a short story she had written for one of the sessions and her instructor told her that she had too much material for a short story and suggested she turn it into a children's mystery novel. Elizabeth followed the instructor's suggestions and a year later had a finished manuscript, *The Ghost Of Padre Island.*

Just before she left on a long trip, she read about a contest sponsored by Abington Press and decided to enter her manuscript. When she came back from the trip she had a letter from Abington. She didn't win the contest, but they wanted to publish her book if she would agree to make certain changes. Since most of the changes were fairly minor she agreed, but there was one chapter, her favorite, that she refused to change.

"I agreed to most of the changes, but when they wanted me to change things about a hurricane and tamper with my beautiful descriptions in that chapter we went back and forth a few times. The editor tried to convince me that this segment slowed down the action and nobody but a fool would stay on Padre Island during a hurricane. I finally compromised and made it a very, very bad storm so my characters could stay on the island and I could keep my nice description.

"My husband and children were very proud when the book came out, but I think my mother was the one who rejoiced the most because she was able to appreciate all of the hard work that goes into the making of a book. I was so glad that it came out while she was alive. The dedication in the book is to Ivy, my mother, and to Velvet, a black basset hound. The dog grew up with my children and played a very prominent part in the story. Some people have asked me if my mother was offended having to share the dedication page with a basset hound. I told them 'certainly not.' She thought as much of that dog as we did.

"My husband wrote and published medical articles and would ask me to help edit them. The fact that I was writing children's books was in no way threatening or competitive with what he was doing."

First Ladies of Texas, Stillhouse Hollow Press, 1976, was published one year after her children's book came out. Here she was again switching back and forth with her writing. One year she produced a children's mystery novel and the next an adult non-fiction book.

She co-authored this book with Mary Farrell, who was a friend and history teacher at Temple Junior College.

"The book was Mary's idea. She had been doing research on the women who were the wives of the Governors and of the Presidents of Texas. She had given a number of speeches about these women and each time someone would ask her why she didn't put all of that information into a book. When she realized there was enough interest in the subject she decided to tackle a book project. Since she was a researcher, she asked me if I would do the writing. When I accepted the challenge I had no idea of what I was getting into. Before the book was finished I had gotten involved in some of the research, but it was a very co-operative venture. Mary was a very, very, wonderful partner to work with.''

While she was doing research for *First Ladies*, she kept run-ning across accounts of a man named Dr. Ashbel Smith. She learned that he had operated on Margaret Houston for a breast tumor and helped Mary Jones publish Anson Jones' book, after Anson Jones committed suicide. He was a close friend and roommate of Sam Houston. His name popped up more and more.

''I definitely became interested in this man and started col-lecting bits and pieces of information about him.''

Even though she wasn't sure just what she should do with the material, Elizabeth, found herself collecting more and more on this man. Little did she know at that time that this project would help her over some of the roughest spots in her life. Her interest and devotion to the research would help her keep her balance when everything around her was crumbling.

When Elizabeth's twenty-four year old son, Steve, was studying microbiology at the University of Texas Medical School in Galveston, he became ill. Since he had a good medical his-tory, they were stunned when they learned that he had Hodg-kin's disease, which was fatal.

''This was a difficult time in our lives and I'm sure that this stress and worry for Steve, contributed to my husband's early death of heart disease. He died of a heart attack in January 1977. My son lived for two years and died in February 1979.

''I took a leave of absence from my teaching job at the Ju-nior College and went to Galveston to help take care of Steven and see that he got good meals during the time he was in treat-ment.

''He was involved in a research project at the medical school and continued his studies after he became ill and seemed to work harder and push himself more during this time.

''There has been an award set up to honor him at the medi-cal school which I'm very proud of. It is *The Stephen Clark Sil-*

verthorne Memorial Award, and is presented to a student who has done outstanding research in the microbiology department of the University of Texas Medical School.''

During this trying time, Elizabeth was able to continue on her writing project. This helped keep her going. She was still collecting data on Ashbel Smith and she started another children's book, *I Heracles.*

''I was working on this book during the time of my son and husband's illness. It came out while my son was ill and I dedicated the book to him because to me Heracles symbolizes the kind of person Steve was. During his illness he had great strength and courage.''

This book was derived because of Elizabeth's continued interest in mythology. She wanted to find a way to make the story come alive for children and not be so formal or stilted. This is the reason she chose to tell the story in first person. To give it more of an emotional impact and more appeal.

''I was trying to make the story as interesting as possible for children. The story tells about each of Heracles twelve adventures when he had to do his twelve labors. Each labor is a separate chapter and is treated as an adventure story for that labor.''

When Elizabeth first started collecting material on Ashbel Smith she had intended to use the material for the article, but the material soon outgrew the article idea and began to develop into a book.

For seven years she followed in the footsteps of Ashbel Smith. Her travels took her to the British Museum in London. To North Carolina where he practiced medicine and taught. She spent time in Paris tracing his life while he was there.

''I have spent a good part of my life in the Barker archives at the University of Texas, where all of Ashbel Smith's personal papers are kept. There are ten feet eight inches of these papers and I have been through this dim, faded, handwritten material piece by piece.

''A lot of people have asked me why I was spending so much time on this project. I admit this had been like an obsession but it has been good for me. With all of the things that's happened in my life, I needed something that I was deeply interested in and something that would absorb my time and energy. I always knew I had this project to turn to. It helped me to survive those tragic filled days and months of my life. The project is finished now and the book, *Ashbel Smith, Pioneer Texan*, will be published by Texas A&M University Press in the spring of 1982.''

Elizabeth did use part of the material that she had collected to write an article on Ashbel Smith for Civil War Times Illustrated. Because of this article a group of doctors in Austin invited her to come and talk to them about the civil war. At first Elizabeth didn't know exactly what to center her speech on, but finally decided to talk about the coastal defense of Texas during the civil war. In preparation for her talk, she became interested in the Texas Navy. She wrote an article about the navy and sold it to Oceans Magazine.

''It took quite a bit of research to write that article, because very few people know much about the Texas Navy. The Navy existed before the civil war and ended when Texas became annexed to the United States.''

Because of her devotion to teaching and to writing, Elizabeth, has achieved an outstanding background in education. She has studied at Rice University, University of Houston, University of Mexico, Queens College, New York; University of Texas, San Miguel de Allende, Mexico; Midwestern University, Breadloaf Writer's School and Temple Buell College, Denver, Colorado.

She holds a BA degree with honors from Texas Women's University, and an MA degree with honors from North Texas State University.

Her deep interest in education and her involvement in writing has led her to the Wordsworth Conference, Lake District, England.

''Richard Wordsworth, the great-great-grandson of William Wordsworth sponsors this conference each year. Richard is an actor and a scholar. He invites renowned authorities on the life and works of Wordsworth to be guest lecturers. This is a tremendous experience in learning.''

In 1980, Elizabeth, participated in the six weeks travel seminar on children's literature sponsored by Fort Hays University in Kansas.

"Donna Harsh, who is with the University at Fort Hays, conducts a study tour each year. There is a very lengthy and detailed study that goes along with the trip. The reading list is pages and pages. I chose to take the course without credit so that I could do as little or as much of the reading as my time would allow me to. We toured Europe and attended planned seminars where international children's authors were the speakers. We met the scholars, the authors and the illustrators of books. Sometimes there were language barriers, but we always had interpreters.

"We went to Germany, Holland, England and Ireland. We saw the place where the Pied Piper was written and many of the places that inspired both the modern authors and the authors of the past such as Hans Christian Andersen, the Grimm's brothers and many others.

"Donna doesn't waste a minute. While we were traveling from place to place, she had planned lectures on the bus. Each student was required to participate in this. I talked to the group about my writing over the bus microphone, while we were rolling through the German countryside."

Elizabeth always carries a notebook and camera to help record the events of her trip. She has traveled extensively in the pursuit of background material for her writing.

She was in Alaska in the summer gathering material on Alaskan folklore.

"I bought all the literature I could find and recorded the tour guides retelling of the Alaskan tales. I took lots of pictures and lots of notes so when I get ready to work I will have quite a bit of material to work with."

Elizabeth is working on a teen-age romance novel set in New Orleans and made a trip there.

"I took all kinds of pictures around Jackson Square where I plan to tell most of the story. The pictures will help me remember what kind of trees, scrubs and flowers grow here. I can see the children playing and I have been using my tape recorder to record the sounds to go with the pictures. This will help set the mood of the story. Whenever I take a trip I always try to soak up as much material as possible and try to be very receptive to new ideas. I have all kinds of impressions of people that I haven't put down into words yet, but they are stored in my mind just waiting for the time they will be needed to make a story complete.

"The traveling is fun and rewarding, but there comes the time when you have to sit down and do the writing. This is never easy. Writing is one of the hardest jobs in the world. When it's time to write, I can always think of so many things to do instead of writing. The house work or the yard work. Anything except getting back to writing. Sometimes writing is almost painful, but it's something that I feel very pressured to do and I'm not happy with myself if I'm not writing. I'm only really content when I'm writing something and am satisfied with it."

One of the things that has been beneficial to Elizabeth has been attending writer's conferences. She does agree that this can be overdone. "A writer must pick and choose and always save time for writing.

"If you live in a small town as I do, where there are not many writers, you need to talk to people who have the same problems you do. So many people assume that you write a book, send it off and the publisher takes it and that's it. You need to talk to people who understand about writing and who can communicate with you about your work.

"There are two key words that I might pass on to anyone who wants to write. One would be to have preseverance. You have to be a person who doesn't give up. With the writing market as tough as it is today, that's extremely important. The other would be to realize that your work is not engraven in stone. Nothing you write is sacred. You must be willing to rewrite. I think good writing is rewriting."

Elizabeth will continue to let the pendulum swing wide in her writing life. Rotating between adult and children's material, always writing about the things that she is interested in, but you can be sure that whatever she writes will be well researched and well written because she is one of Texas' true scholars and writers.

Nilah Rodgers Turner

6

Nilah Rodgers Turner

"I was a fearless newspaper writer, striking out for justice. My Dad always said I would charge hell with a bucket of water."

Nilah Rodgers was relaxing in her living room in Littlefield, Texas, watching Bob Hope present awards to some outstanding athletes on his, Salute to Young Americans television special. When a young, handsome retarded boy, Brian Loeb stepped on stage to accept the swimming championship award, in the Special Olympics, Nilah's journalistic juices surged and she grabbed a pencil and paper, recognizing a story idea immediately.

As soon as the boy had received his award, Nilah switched off the television and picked up the telephone receiver. Within an hour she had telephoned the boy's mother in Los Angeles, California, to set up a personal interview.

Since her husband was just about to leave on a fishing trip to Mexico, Nilah talked him into dropping her off in Los Angeles. She didn't even have time to get a query in the mail to see if any editor would be interested in this story. But her journalistic instincts proved beneficial and she completed the interview, wrote the article and sold it to Good Housekeeping Magazine.

Because of this article, she received the 1981 Special Olympics Communications Award.

"Perhaps I have more confidence in myself than I deserve, but I just set out strictly on faith. To me ideas absolutely abound out there. It just takes a stupendous amount of nerve and belief in your ability to take off to the east coast or the west coast in pursuit of a story."

But Nilah has not always been in fast pursuit of a story. When she was growing up in the small West Texas town of Littlefield, she had no idea that she would someday be traveling across America writing true life dramas.

"When I was in elementary and high school, I didn't have the faintest inkling that I had what it took to be a writer."

At seventeen, shortly after graduating from high school, Nilah married and embarked on a new life, that of a farmer's wife.

"We only moved eighteen miles from Littlefield, but to me that was a drastic move. From city gal to farm wife was a bit overwhelming at first."

But it didn't take her long to adjust and begin to discover many hidden talents and abilities.

"At first, before I learned better, I used to help my husband with some of the chores. One year I had to help with the cotton crop. My job was to throw the cotton back after it came up through this little spout at the back of the tractor. You have to throw it back into the trailer, stomp it down and then haul it to the gin. We made a great crop that year. That cotton poured through that little spout like liquid gold. Sometimes we'd get as many as two or three bails of cotton on the trailer, then I'd hook the trailer to the pickup truck and haul it to the gin and back I'd come for another load.

"We were almost through with the harvest when they called and said they needed me at the gin to type up government loans. My husband hired two Mexican aliens to take my place and neither one of them could drive. I told him that was the end of me working for him. It took two men to take my place and he still didn't have a hand to haul the cotton to the gin."

As Nilah fulfilled her duties on the farm and started her family she was an insatiable reader.

"I devoured the Reader's Digest, the women's magazines

and even the farm magazines. In lieu of anything else to read, I'd read the back of the cereal box every morning. In those days I had no idea that just anybody could write and get paid for it. My idea of a writer was someone who lived in New York City in a brownstone. But the more I read the more I began to come away with the feeling that I could have written that.''

One day Nilah was reading the Farm Journal and saw a letter written by a schoolteacher's wife, who lived in a town about twenty miles away. What caught her eye was that this letter had a view and an opinion. This started her thinking about some of the funny things that had happened to her since she'd tried to make the transition from city gal to farmer's wife. She whipped out a one-page expose, *Which End Is Up?* and sent it to the Farm Journal.

A few weeks later the piece was returned with a long note from the women's editor. Nilah was crushed, but lack of confidence was not one of her weaknesses. After reading over the article, she still felt it was good, but did rework it a bit and off it went to another magazine, Progressive Farmer. About the time she had forgotten about sending the article, a long flat envelope arrived. Inside was a check for $45.00 and a note thanking her for her contribution and asking her to submit something else.

''Well, they needn't have asked me to submit something else, because prior to this the last job I had paid fifty cents an hour, and I'd spent about an hour on this article and they paid me $45.00. I knew I'd be sending them something else.''

This was the beginning of Nilah's love affair with writing. In the next few years she learned a lot about the technique of writing, but in the beginning she just wrote what she felt.

When Johnson was President and received so much publicity about pulling his beagle's ears and when Nilah learned that Lucy Johnson had a collie, she was in the writing business again. It just happened that she had a beagle, a collie and was a democrat. So she rolled another piece of paper in the typewriter and wrote about going to town with her beagle and collie and being mistaken for Lucy Johnson.

I've Gone To The Dogs, brought her another check for $45.00. Since she was fast becoming a published writer, she felt she needed to get busy and learn some of the basic skills of her chosen trade. Since her three sons were in school she decided to enroll in the nearby community college.

"When I decided to go to college I picked out the toughest English teacher and enrolled in her class. In this class if you made one mistake you got a B, two a C, three a D and four an F. This teacher was a real toughie. But this was what I needed. I really wanted to learn. When she gave us an assignment to write a character sketch, I wrote about our school superintendent because he was the most interesting man I had ever met. I put a lot of time in on the assignment and looked up almost every word I wrote, wanting the sketch to be perfect, but I misspelled the word among, of all things. I put a U instead of an O. Not just once, but three times. The teacher gave me a D and I was just killed because I thought I had done a good job and deserved a better grade."

Because she had put so much work in on the assignment, she began to look around for a place to market it, and decided that it would be something the newspapers might like to have. She didn't send it to just one, but to three papers.

"I sent the article to the Littlefield, Loveland and Lubbock papers and they all printed it on page one. They made such a to-do about the article, that I guess I got printer's ink in my veins right then."

Nilah's writing really took off after that. She began to write more and more articles for the farm magazines.

"My first few articles were funny, but then I guess I lost my funny bone. I must have said all I had to say that was funny and I got serious."

When Nilah moved to the farm as a young bride she knew nothing of farm life, but because of her well-written articles to some of the farm magazines, she began to get assignments from them, asking her to write highly technical articles about farmers, the method and equipment they used. Each assignment was a real challenge and Nilah's nerve and confidence in her own ability helped her accept these challenges and with each assignment completed, she was fast becoming an expert in the farming community. She wrote hundreds of these technical farm articles.

These articles paved the way to another writing adventure, that of public relations work.

"I worked for Elanco and several other companies for a couple of years. They paid me $200 a day plus expenses to do almost the same thing I was doing for the farm magazines. I became quite an expert on farming before we left the country and moved back to town."

Later Nilah went to work for the *Levelland Daily News.* "I worked on the paper for ten years and that was about nine years too long."

While at the paper she held many different positions, but the one she disliked the most was when she was women's editor. She would knock her work out as soon as possible and head for the courthouse to cover the trials.

Late one Saturday afternoon her editor called and said they were putting the paper together and he couldn't find her wedding write-ups. Nilah knew right where they were. They were tucked away in her desk drawer not even written up. She had to go to the office that night and finish her work because she had spent the entire week doing court reporting.

While she was working for the paper, she free-lanced some of her feature articles to Grit, national news magazine, the Sunday supplements and continued to sell to the farm magazines.

"All the time I'd been editing and writing for the paper I would bring my problems home and regularly my husband would say, 'Why don't you quit that darn newspaper?' The year after we'd lost money farming three years in a row and got hailed out the next two, I came home one day and announced that I was quitting the paper.

"My timing was so colossal that I had to make it free-lancing. All these years I had been writing about people, but only superficially. Now I could spend the time I needed to really do in-depth stories."

By this time Nilah had been to a few writer's conferences and had heard one of the editors from Reader's Digest say that the best way to break into the Digest was to do a drama in real life. Two days before her job ended at the newspaper, she was eating lunch and listening to the Texas news on the radio. There was a story about a Texas rancher who had saved the lives of three airmen whose helicopter had crashed on his ranch. All afternoon this story kept running through Nilah's mind. When she got home that evening she telephoned the rancher and set up an interview. This was her first attempt at writing a true life drama.

While interviewing the rancher she learned that he had a college degree and fancied himself writing the story as well as she could and because of her inexperience she let him talk her into splitting her fee with him 50/50.

"That was the end of my splitting fees. If anyone asks me if I split fees I now have a stock answer. I tell them fee splitting is something doctor's do. I had to learn the hard way that the average person cannot put a story together. Without the foresight and hard work of the writer and their expertise in finding a market, most stories would probably never be told."

When Nilah completed the story of the rescue she sent it to Elaine Franklin at Reader's Digest. It wasn't long before she had it back with a note asking for revisions.

"I wrote and rewrote that story until my file looked more like a novel than a 2,500 word article, but I finally got it right and *Rescue On The Pedernales,* was a reality."

Her next article was also a true life drama about a young woman who had lost her husband in an auto accident and had been left terribly disfigured. Because she had two young twin daughters she had fought a hard battle to stay alive. *Is That You Mommy?* was sold to Good Housekeeping Magazine.

After that the true life drama became Nilah's first love. She wrote and sold so many stories to Good Housekeeping, with a Texas background, that Jean Block had to start turning them down with the comment that 'G.H. couldn't OD on Texas.'

"After this I knew I had to expand my horizons."

The next year she took a long interview trip to the east coast. The year after that she went to the west coast. Through these ramblings she gathered enough material for many articles. She sold well over 200 articles to major magazines. Ten of these went to Good Housekeeping, one to Ladies' Home Journal and six to Reader's Digest.

"I'm known at G.H. and the Digest as a ''disaster'' writer.
I like the stories with ordeals, the moving real life drama that
present personal traumas. I like the personal warmth, the courage displayed and the triumps over adversity.''

Although Nilah has not had any medical training, most of
her major articles have been medical in one respect or another.

''There is real built-in drama in traumatic situations that
happen in the twinkling of an eye which change a person's life
forever. I've written about so many amputations and operations
that I feel like I've been in intensive care for these four or five
years I've been free-lancing full time.''

One of the editor's at the Digest told Nilah that she was
the only person, except Joan Mills, who had ever sold the Digest
six articles in one year.

When Nilah realized that she would have to broaden her
horizon if she continued to sell true life dramas, her ever present
nerve and belief in herself helped her take off to New York and
points east.

''I didn't have one firm assignment. I just had a tentative
go ahead from Reader's Digest and Good Housekeeping editors. With no more than just an invitation to drop by for lunch
while I was in New York.

''I always set up my interviews ahead of time. Then just as
soon as I leave an interview I make a very short outline. Putting
down the theme, how many scenes and what viewpoint I intend
to use. Then I forget that interview until I get ready to write the
story. If the people are not reluctant, I use a tape recorder, but I
always take notes. Sometimes I listen to the tape when I get
ready to do the story, but not always. The tape is very handy to
catch inflections of tone and to fill in the gaps when you can't
read your notes.''

As Nilah's career began to build she learned of a writer's
group in Lubbock and decided that she needed to be associated
with other working writers. Through this group she met Etta
Lynch and Wanda Evans.

''Etta deserves a medal. She's very, very helpful. She's
been very generous with her time and goes out of her way to
help. We've co-authored several articles together.''

While attending a workshop in Lubbock, Nilah became acquainted with the featured speaker, Louise Boggess, who is a writer and teacher from San Matel, California.

"Louise has been very helpful in critiquing some of my manuscripts. I don't always do as she suggests, but I always listen.

"I had written a story about a young boy who had saved his father's life and sent it to Louise for her opinion. She thought the story was good, but told me I shouldn't write the story from the boy's viewpoint because it would limit the market. She felt that none of the major magazines would use a story written from a boy's viewpoint. But that was the only way the story would work so I stuck to my guns on that one and sold it to Reader's Digest.

"Louise was right about limiting your market when you write from this viewpoint or even from the male's viewpoint. I really think about six times before I use either of these viewpoints, but you must do the story from the viewpoint of the person who makes the sacrifice. The one who learns the lesson."

When Nilah quit her job at the newspaper, she gave herself one year to make it free-lancing. At the end of that year, she decided to try to double her production the next year.

"It would be hard for me to go back to a 9-5 job. I really like being able to work at home, at my own pace. I'm sure I have more confidence than talent. I belong to the class A personality and I'm determined to achieve in whatever field I tackle. I'm highly competitive. If I were playing cards for matches, I'd want to win all the matches. I was a fearless newspaper writer, striking out for justice. My dad always said that I would charge hell with a bucket of water. I welcome the slower pace of the human interest drama. I'll never go back to straight journalism.

"Being competitive, aggressive and going at everything in a "make or break" attitude and wanting to be in control and call the shots are not always pluses. I guess I have several "warts." If I didn't have anyone else to compete with, I'd compete against myself.

"If I did five pages yesterday, I'd try for ten today and if I got ten today, I'd try for fifteen tomorrow. I like to succeed at whatever I'm doing, whether it's writing or baking a cake."

Nilah's husband is her number one fan. Her boys take what she does for granted. They can't remember a time when their mother wasn't writing.

"I was over at my Dad's a few days ago and he said, 'What kind of poop are you working on now?' To him my writing is just poop, but he loves me and thinks anything I do is just great.

"When I'm working, I work like a Turk. That's the only way I could have sold those six stories to Readers' Digest in one year. That was the only year I could have done that because right after I sold those stories the magazine became overstocked. They started moving editor's around and made all kinds of changes.

"When I got home from my trip to the east coast I just knocked those stories out as fast as I could. I would rewrite and polish and do everything possible to get them finished and in the mail.

"The first story I wrote from that trip was, *It Won't Hurt Because You're My Brother.* This was about a little boy who had given his brother a kidney. I was a bit pressured to get this story finished and sold. I knew if the boy died before the story was published there wouldn't be a story, but the boy didn't die and is still alive today."

Because of this article Nilah was invited to Washington, D.C. to receive an award from the National Kidney Foundation.

In 1980, she received the Leroy Wolfe Communications Award (later renamed The National Cystic Fibrosis Award). In 1981 she received the Special Olympics Communications award and The National Kidney Foundation Award.

Nilah has always approached her writing like a professional. To her, writing is a job and has priority over some minor chores. She keeps regular working hours as she did when she was holding down a job. A typical work day is from 10-5.

"I put off housekeeping chores except making beds and straightening every morning until I've completed my work at the typewriter. I'm not a very organized person. My desk is almost always cluttered. If it is in order that means I'm between projects. When I'm knee deep in an article I have my notes spread all over my desk."

Her huge antique desk is facing a wall to help block out

distractions. There are little maxims and bits of wisdom thumb-tacked over her desk.

"I'm a little like the legendary ship captain. Every morning his first mate watched him go into his cabin and reverently bow before the safe. Almost as though he were in prayer, he withdrew a slip of paper and in a very pious position read the words he held before him. One morning the first mate came in and found the captain keeled over before the safe. The great captain had suffered a heart attack. The first mate searched the captain's pockets until he found the tiny piece of paper with the combination to the safe and with trembling fingers began to spin the dial until the safe opened. At last he could avail himself of the wisdom and knowledge that made his captain the master of the seas. Hardly breathing, he took out the paper that held such awe and such reverence and his eyes caught sight of the few words scribbled on the paper.

STARBOARD — RIGHT; PORTSIDE — LEFT.

"That's the way I operate. I look up over my typewriter and read: A STORY IS AN EMOTION, NOT A RECORD OF FACT. EVERY SCENE ENDS WITH THE ILLUSTRATION OF YOUR THEME.

I have a little 3 x 5 card that reminds me that every story must have situation, a complication, a crisis and a resolution. Above that I keep a simplified plotting outline: OPENING SCENE (PRESENT STRONG PROBLEM — AIM FOR THE HEART). SUBJECTIVE PROBLEM — OBJECTIVE PROBLEM —FLASHBACK—FIRST COMPLICATION—SECOND COMPLICATION — SACRIFICE — REWARD.

"I know all of these things, but sometimes I have to remind myself. Sometimes I stick that little 3 x 5 card in my pocket while I'm walking around the park or in my purse when I'm waiting for an appointment. Then when I get back to my desk I know which is starboard and which is portside."

Because she has treated her writing like a profession, her daughters-in-law and other family members have treated it with some degree of respect. They preface their requests for her to babysit or help them with the phrase, "Are you busy?"

"If I'm truly busy, I tell them so. If I'm retyping a manuscript or doing something that can be picked up at any time, I'll stop. After all, my grandchildren, like my children, will be babies just once. Besides, I can think and bake cookies at the same time.

"To accomplish anything you've got to concentrate your efforts and attention. If you have an intense, unwavering determination to make your objectives and goals a reality, nothing can stop you. You must learn to focus your attention on your goals if you want to succeed. Where one succeeds because of genius or brilliance, ten succeed because of persistence. Persistent people begin their success where others end in failure."

Because Nilah has taken her own advise, applied her talent, set goals and had the determination and persistence to follow through, she has become a prolific writer.

Her Texas heritage and her never failing nerve and belief in her own ability has provided her with a rewarding life as a non-fiction writer.

Dorothy Prunty

7

Dorothy Prunty

"I think I'm living one of the greatest times of my life right now and my writing is the main force that's creating such excitement and new life."

After a rewarding career as a teacher, Dorothy Prunty found another career quite by accident. Her oldest daughter, Gail, came home from college one week end very excited. She told her mother that she had sold an article to the Chamber of Commerce magazine in Austin, as a result of one of her assignments in her journalism class.

"Mother, I don't understand why you don't write. You've had so many experiences. You lived abroad during World War II and you've traveled so much. Why in the world don't you write?"

Late Sunday afternoon after her daughter left for college, Dorothy, began to think about her comments.

"At that time my husband was extremely busy. He was county auditor and operated our two large ranches. Even though I held a full time teaching job, I still had lots of time to myself."

That very afternoon Dorothy sat down and wrote her first article. She didn't draw from her vast traveling experiences or rely on her memory of living abroad during the war or depend on her tenure as a Red Cross Worker to furnish her information for the article. Instead, she chose to write about an incident closer to home.

Her story was about how her minister, Bill Murray, had inspired community action with a sermon. As a result of this ser-

mon several programs were initiated including a hospital auxiliary, a day care center and a summer recreation program.

After she completed the story she titled it, *The Unfolding
Miracle,* and sent it to the Methodist publication, *The Interpreter.* Within a month she had a check for $35.00 and a re-
quest to submit another article.

"If that check had been for $3500, it couldn't have thrilled
me more. That sale launched a new career for me."

That first check came in the fall and by the end of the year,
Dorothy had written and sold ten articles.

"It was amazing that I started out so well. After I came
home from school every day, I would grab an apple and after relaxing a bit head for the typewriter. I tried to spend at least an
hour writing. My husband didn't get in until dark, so I had
plenty of time for this new venture.

"All of a sudden my writing began to mean more to me
than just about anything. With both of my daughters in college
and my husband busy running two ranches, I really needed
something that would give me a new excitement and writing
proved to be the stabilizing force which I needed at that time."

Dorothy describes herself as "a late life writer," but her
whole life had been in preparation for her second career.

Her Aunt was a writer and sold many stories to Cosmopolitan and other popular women's magazines. The family always
celebrated those sales and even as a small child, Dorothy thought
that writing must be the most exciting profession in the world.

When she was in elementary school she kept her classmates
entertained with her storytelling.

In high school she wrote a fiction story, entered it in a contest sponsored by The Decatur Texas Owl Club and won the first
prize which was $5.00.

It was years before she would take up her pen and begin to
write again. After completing her education at North Texas
State University in Denton, she taught one term in Lawton,
Oklahoma. In 1941 she quit her teaching job and went to the
Panama Canal Zone as a civil service worker. She joined the Red
Cross while there and was sent to Tyler, Texas, for training.

While she was training in Tyler, she met Luther Prunty

who was in the hospital recovering from malaria. He had survived three and a half years as a Japanese POW.

After Dorothy and Luther were married they settled in his hometown of Jacksboro. They began their family and Dorothy entered the teaching profession again.

"Luther is kind of a romantic character to a lot of people because he is a cowboy. My daughter, Marsha, wrote a story about her daddy comparing him to the disco cowboy. She told about all the different things that make up real ranch living. Her daddy might be out pulling a calf at five in the morning or be involved in vaccinating, spraying or riding fence. He is quite a contrast to the disco cowboy because he is a real working cowboy."

Even though Luther is a working cowboy and oversees two large ranches, in partnership with another man, Dorothy's life has remained unattached to ranch life.

"We've really traveled different roads. Luther insisted that I get my masters. It's made a big difference financially and even though I didn't need to teach for economic reasons, I felt it was something I should do. Luther has a very high IQ. He's a very bright man and very successful. As our daughter, Gail, said, 'We have degrees, but daddy has the smarts.'

After Dorothy had sold to most of the religious and educational markets, she began to look around for something different and decided to try writing profiles. She wanted to find exciting people, doing unusual things and tell their story. To her amazement she uncovered a vast array of people fitting her requirements right in her own hometown.

Rev. Harold Black, a Presbyterian minister, was featured in an article published in *The Interpreter*. This article was about his involvement in the Laubach Literacy Program.

Five-Six, a Methodist youth publication printed the story of Sarah Price, Margaret Hendricks, Carolyn Lindsey and Donna Henderson who were working on the God and Community award in Girl Scouts.

Joe Paul Nichols, whose record, *Hello Trouble*, was a hit on the country-western charts was the subject of Dorothy's article,

Country Music — Country Boy, published in Modern People magazine.

She wrote about Jerry Sharp and the annual rattlesnake safari in *Snakes Alive* which sold to Scholastic magazine.

After selling more than one hundred articles, Dorothy took early retirement in order to devote more time to writing.

"Even though I haven't sold to all of the top markets, I've sold to some and not a two-week period goes by without at least one sale."

In 1975 before her retirement from her twenty-seven years of teaching, she was named the *Outstanding Elementary Teacher of America,* a national honor.

"My principal nominated me for this award because he was impressed with the creative writing program I had developed. The fact that I had sold articles to almost every educational magazine was also a deciding factor."

At a time when some people would be thinking about sitting back and basking in their past glory, Dorothy, was embarking on a new career, one which she felt would be even more rewarding than the first.

But not everything Dorothy writes finds a home the first time out. She has had a few setbacks. When she sent one of her articles to the West Texas Chamber of Commerce magazine, she got a scathing letter from the editor, instead of the $25.00 check she was hoping for.

"This editor not only attacked my manuscript, he attacked me. He said I should not even write anymore. It was terrible. But by this time I had learned to treat my writing as a business. I had a product to sell and if this editor didn't want to buy the product someone else would."

Without making one change in this manuscript, Dorothy shuffled it into a fresh envelope, and shot it off to Jimmy Banks, editor, of the *Texas Star.*

"The famous Jimmy Banks called me on the telephone and said he wanted to buy the article. He wanted a bit more information, but basically the article was fine the way it was. *The Hoot Owl,* was published in the *Texas Star* and he paid me $175.

"When you're writing you have to learn to accept rejection. That's part of the business. You're selling something and if one editor doesn't want it there's no reason to take it personal and get your feelings hurt. Most editors are not like the editor who wrote that scathing letter. It's not you, the editors are rejecting or it shouldn't be. Usually the article doesn't fit in with what they are doing at the time. I never let a rejected manuscript lay around very long. I send it out again right away.''

When Dorothy went back to North Texas State University for her masters she was told that she made one of the highest scores ever made on the master's entrance exam. Her principal learned later that her score was so high that it shook the faculty at the University.

Even though she scored 98% on her writing ability, one of her Professors called her into his office near the end of her degree program and said, ''Mrs. Prunty, even though you made a 98% on writing ability on your entrance exam, I haven't seen any indication of your writing ability. I just don't think you can write well at all.'' Dorothy didn't let this shake her, she looked the Professor straight in the eye and replied, ''Well, that's your opinion.''

''I've often wished that I could go back over there and stack all of my published work on his desk.''

With her constant sales and her versatility as a writer, Dorothy has proven over and over again that this Professor was wrong in his evaluation of her writing ability.

She is constantly on the lookout for possible article ideas and has developed a keen sense of awareness to the people and activities around her. From the 3500 people living in her hometown, she has already written more than seventeen profiles, spotlighting these interesting people or their activities and continues to look for new material among the local town folks.

Some local residents who were trained and encouraged to excel in a golfing career by Henry J. Richards was the subject of her article, *The Town That Grows Golfers,* and published in the *Wichita Falls Record News.*

''In a period of about ten years, Jacksboro produced about ten pro-golfers. Rik and Don Massengale won the Bob Hope Tournament. While I was writing this article I got an idea for another one. Later I wrote about Rik Massengale's religious experience and called it *Golf Or God.*"

Another article, *He Calls Them Square,* Modern People Magazine, was about a man who was a square dance caller and had several gold records to his credit. This article was rewritten as *Square Dance Caller* and sold to The State magazine.

Dorothy gets as much mileage as possible out of her material. It isn't unusual for her to sell each of her articles four or five times.

Other interesting subjects who live in or near her hometown are Jackie Worthington, a champion woman rodeo star.

"Jackie's won more awards in the women's division than anyone in the world. She has been inducted into the Cowgirl Hall of Fame in Kerrville, Texas. She's retired now and runs a ranch here. I've sold her story several times."

The local Postmaster's unusual hobby of raising exotic birds was another interesting story which sold to Farm & Ranch Living and brought Dorothy a check for $300.

She told the story of Ida Mae Stark, a local resident who makes $7,000 wedding cakes and sold it to the *Houston Post's* Sunday supplement magazine.

"I try to sell every article at least four or five times. I look for ideas that I know will sell a lot of different ways. Of course, you have to slant the material to fit each publication.

"When I was in Denmark on a trip, I became interested in their Danish Christmas spoons. These spoons are very unusual and I thought this would be a piece that I could sell many times.

"The first time I wrote the article I slanted it toward people who would be interested in the spoons as an investment. Rarities magazine bought the article for their December 1981 issue. Then I rewrote the article slanting it toward the Danes themselves. I knew the Danes would be more interested in the craftmanship and have a very patriotic view of the spoons. My second sale was to the American Danish Society magazine for their December 1982 issue."

After reslanting and adding fresh anecdotes, she expects to get several more sales from the Danish spoons material.

"When I'm traveling I make lots of notes. After I get back

home I reassemble the notes and file them away. Later I may go back through them looking for ideas.''

During the early forties, Dorothy lived and worked in the Panama Canal Zone. Later she made two trips to Europe, and has visited the Orient, South America, Mexico, Canada, Guatemala, Hawaii, New Zealand, Australia, Java, Singapore, Thailand and the Philippines.

''When I was In Taiwan I was very impressed with a marble bridge that was built way up in the mountains. I kept thinking and thinking about that bridge. Finally I went through my notes to see what information I had on the bridge and found enough to write, *The Bridge of Motherly Devotion,* and sold it to an Asian magazine.

''I've discovered that the tape recorder is a handy and valuable tool to take on a trip. The first time I used the tape recorder was in the fall of 1981 when I visited Big Bend National Park. I taped most of the guide's talks and that was so good because when I got home and started to write my article I had all of the straight dope. I sold that article to Virginia Allen, editor, for the Lufkin Line magazine.''

In the fall of 1981, with her husband, and a group of former POW's and their wives, Dorothy made a trip retracing the course of the men's internment. Her husband was captured in Java, taken to Singapore, worked on the railroad and the bridge on the river Kwai and was finally released in Bangkok, Thailand.

''This was a very emotional trip. If I don't write about some of those experiences, I should have my head examined. In Bangkok, we were invited into a Chinese home and were served snails. That was quite an experience.

''We went to New Zealand and then on to the POW convention in Sidney, Australia. The trip was carefully planned and when we went into Indonesia some of the senators had written ahead and gotten permission for us to go into the camp where these men had been stationed before their capture. It's now an Indonesian army camp.

''When we were in Australia we were invited into the home

of a man who had lost his arm while carrying supplies to a gun implacement position, near the river Kwai.

"This man lives in a condo and invited us to dinner. After we had eaten, some of the neighbors came over to meet the "Texans."

"One woman came in carrying a copy of the Texas Highways magazine and when I told her one of my articles was scheduled for that magazine she said, 'how wonderful.' She was very excited to hear this. I wish that my article could have been in the issue she had."

There have been many side rewards in Dorothy's career as a writer. When she wrote the article, *Typing Their Way To Language Skills,* Instructor magazine, she was bombarded with letters wanting more information.

"This story was about a teacher who developed a system of teaching her students language art skills on the typewriter. Their spelling improved 30% using this method. I understand that her school got even more request for additional information than I did. That was a very successful article."

She did a story about a man in Jacksboro who developed an unusual okra strain and sold it to Gardens For All. This okra grows six to seven feet tall and is very tender. The man told Dorothy that he would send seeds to anyone requesting them. The response for seed was overwhelming and after over two hundred letters requesting the seeds, he ran out.

"The magazine staff decided that they should do a brochure and spotlight this man. This was so good because he has terrible arthritis and is in constant pain. All this attention really gave him a new lease on life."

This man is still reaping the delightful rewards of that article. A man in Alaska killed a strange bird and found some seeds in his craw. He had read Dorothy's article about the man and his okra and sent these seeds to this man in Jacksboro.

When Dorothy wrote about a veterinarian, Dr. Young, who did acupuncture on animals, to help relieve their pain, she received money in his behalf.

"The article didn't ask for money, but a lot of people were so touched by this man's compassion for animals that they sent him money to help in his research. When I got the money, I just put it in an envelope and mailed it to him.''

It appears that Dorothy has an uncanny ability for finding stories in her own backyard.

As she became more and more interested in writing, she began to look around for fellow writers so she could talk shop. She found such a group meeting in a neighboring town of Springtown.

''Most of the people who were in that group were non-fiction writers. I went to their meetings for a couple of years. One writer, Wynelle Catlin was more interested in writing children's books. We became good friends and encouraged each other when we hit a low point. Wynelle wrote the book, *Old Wattles*, published by Doubleday. She was a good influence on me, but she moved to Dallas and I felt like I was in the middle of the desert with no other writers around that I could relate to, until I met Bernice Maddock.

''I was so delighted to meet her. She lives out in the country near Weatherford. She writes lots of inspirational and humor articles. These are the kinds of articles that don't need much research and she makes about $250 on each of them. She just recently sold five and has the lead article in the November 1981 Ideals magazine. Bernice has really been an inspiration to me. I'm glad I found her.

''As long as I write, I sell. My percentage of sales is very high. I sell enough to supplement my income and keep my morale up. I make just about the same with my writing as I did when I was teaching.''

When Dorothy speaks at Writer's Conferences and Teacher's In-Service Workshops, she always brings a spark of excitement with her. She tells her audience, 'I'm living one of the greatest times of my life right now and my writing is the main force that's creating such excitement and new life.' She throws out a challenge to the teachers to start writing and encourages the aspiring writer to get busy and write and rewrite and then to submit their work and expect it to sell.

''When you are writing non-fiction a query is a must.'' ''It should be brief but interesting.''

When querying the editor at Arizona Highways about an idea, she tried to grab his attention in the first two paragraphs.

"A new brand of lawman watches over Arizona's desert areas. He's known as a cactus cop.

"The pilferage of the cactus plant by truckloads created the need for the guardians of the desert. They come at night, seeking the saquaro giant which will bring forty dollars each at some markets."

The editor, Tom Cooper, returned the query with a brief handwritten note at the bottom.

"I'm interested, but it must be Arizona exclusively, and authoritative!"

When she first began writing, her husband's attitude toward this new career was negative, but as Dorothy became more and more involved, his attitude changed. He was indirectly responsible for her writing and publishing a poem.

"At first, Luther thought that my writing would cause such a stir that people would laugh at me, but when he realized the type of writing I was doing his attitude changed. He was proud of the things I was writing. He bought me two real good cameras to use in my work. I was experimenting with one of the cameras and took a difficult night shot of one of the lighted stained glass windows in our church. The picture came out better than I had expected so I just jotted down a poem to go with the picture and sent it to Response magazine. They bought it and printed the picture and the poem on the inside of the cover. An Easter Prayer, was my first and only published poem."

Dorothy entered her second career with great excitement and high expectations and she has not lost that zest and anticipation for finding good story material.

"I'm always looking for ideas. When I get an idea I go after it with break-neck speed. Oh, I get high on ideas."

With her car gassed up, her tape recorder in hand and her camera loaded, she is off on another interview trip to Buffalo, Texas, to interview the man who manages a herd of Texas Longhorn cattle. You can be sure that she will make this story work for her and will find several ready markets.

In a very short time Dorothy Prunty has become one of Texas' most prolific non-fiction writers.

8

Margaret Cousins

(Mary Parrish - William Masters - Avery Johns)

"I never confused my work with literature. I was always writing for entertainment."

Margaret Cousins was born January 26, 1906, in Munday, a small prairie town in West Texas.

"I was born on the Knox prairie in a big brass bed at home. I didn't know another child until I was five when my brother was born."

From that small town in Texas, Maggie's imaginative ideas and ambitions were to take her through many successful years as a writer and editor for some of the most prestigious magazine and book publishers in New York City. Her career path was to change many times, but her keen perception and her dedication to her chosen profession, helped her make many difficult decisions.

The first of those decisions came in 1936, while the country was still in the great depression and when it was considered "scandalous" for a single woman to leave home and live alone, Maggie, packed her bags and headed for New York City.

"It took me three months to get out of town. My parents thought my leaving was terrible. 'Going up there to live by herself!' It was like somebody had died around our house."

Her parents left her in New York City only after they were assured that she would be well chaperoned by Herbert Mayes, a family friend and her new employer.

"Herbert Mayes didn't have time to chaperon me. He was the editor of the Pictorial Review magazine and it was in trou-

Margaret Cousins

ble. He spent most of his time trying to save the magazine. Besides, he had a family of his own to look after. He left me pretty much to myself and that was fine with me.

"I had a wonderful time that first year. I didn't know anybody in New York. My job was to read the unsolicited mail and that was all, so I was through every day by five thirty. We had a tremendous volume of poetry because we had a man who read poetry over the radio. It wasn't unusual to get ten thousand poems a month. Of course, I couldn't read every word of all of them, but you don't have to eat the whole egg to find out that it's bad.

"I had a ball that first year. I took in the six day bicycle races, went to Madison Square Gardens, and saw all musical theater. For fifty-five cents you could get a seat in the peanut roof. That's all I could afford, but I loved it and couldn't have been happier."

But because of the "economic spur," Maggie had to stop some of her endless wanderings and turn her mind back to writing.

"It was either write or starve to death. I could never just work at one thing. I always had to combine writing and editing to keep myself going."

But writing was not a new venture for Maggie. She had been writing most of her life. At four, when her peers were playing wth dolls and making mud cakes, Maggie was listening to her father read O'Henry stories. By the time she was five she had learned to write. At six, when most children are just beginning to be exposed to the academic world, Maggie was already writing stories. When she was fourteen she wrote a poem about Rudolph Valentino and sold it to the Motion Picture magazine.

"My father always read aloud to my brother and me. He read everything from the complete works of Edgar Allen Poe to the Saturday Evening Post. He read nine volumes of the short stories of O'Henry to us. I believe this is why I became a short story writer."

Maggie's family moved from Munday, Texas, when she was five and after a brief stay in Wichita Falls, they settled in Dallas. When Maggie finished high school in Dallas, she entered the University of Texas hoping for a career as an architect, but she soon abandoned this idea.

"Since I couldn't pass freshman math and couldn't draw very well, I knew being an architect was out of the question. I took freshman math four times and still couldn't get it. When they called me up before the math board, I thought I was really in trouble. They wanted to know what was wrong with the math department when nobody could teach me enough math to pass. They told me that I was apparently a highly intelligent woman and they just couldn't understand this math block. They transferred me to the football section so I could graduate.

"Some of my trouble began when I was a young child. I was near-sighted and couldn't see the board. Nobody knew it then and that is the reason I never had a good background in math. I just never learned it as a child."

Maggie freely admits that she still has trouble keeping her check book straight.

In 1936, after graduating with a bachelor of arts degree, Maggie, went home to begin her writing and editing career as associate editor for the Southern Pharmaceutical Journal, a trade publication, edited by her father, Walter Cousins, Sr.

"My father started life as a cow puncher. He left home when he was fifteen and worked for the M & M Ranch in the panhandle. He never got out of the third grade, but even though he didn't have any formal education, he was extremely well read. He became a pharmacist and later started the trade journal. By the time I had finished work at the University, he was getting tired of keeping his nose to the grindstone. He wanted to spend some of his time working on the Cowboy's Reunion, so he turned most of the duties of the magazine over to me."

Even though she had most of the responsibility of the publication, she was not always able to get some of her own writing into print. She had learned marketing at the University and started sending some of her overflow material to editors in New York City.

"I wrote a sonnet about some of the people working in a drugstore. The counter man, the messenger boy and the druggist. In those days drugstores were fascinating places. They were chock-full of human interest.

"When my father refused to print these sonnets, I shipped them off to Herbert Mayes, who was then the associate editor for the American Druggist magazine."

Several weeks later Maggie received a phone call from Herbert Mayes. He had read the sonnets and thought they were good, but unfortunately his magazine didn't print verse. He asked Maggie if she could write prose.

"I can write anything for money!"

Because of these sonnets and her apparent ability as a writer, Maggie was given her first assignment. Mr. Mayes sent her to Uvalde, Texas, to interview John Garner's druggist. John Garner was vice-president at that time.

"The very next weekend, I loaded up my Chevy and headed for Uvalde to get the interview. He paid me fifty dollars for that article."

Through the next few years, Maggie, "batted" around on weekends writing on assignment and looking for story material. Most of her associates and friends were obsessed with the fact that she was not married. Everywhere she went someone phrased the same old worn out question. "Maggie, when are you going to settle down and get married?"

She got so tired of hearing this, that she decided to put a stop to it once and for all. It took her quite awhile to devise a plan to cure this situation, but she finally came up with one. She was on the train going home from an assignment when she met up with a judge in her hometown. In the course of the conversation he asked her the same old question, "Maggie, when are you going to find a good man and settle down?" Maggie was ready with her plan. She looked the judge square in the eye and told him quite calmly, "I have decided to take a lover instead."

This story was quickly circulated in her hometown. "My mother was horrified that I would tell the judge something like this, but I never had any trouble about my marriage status after that."

One of Maggie's biggest regrets in life is that she doesn't have children. At one time she had been engaged to a young doctor. Their engagement and approaching wedding plans had already been announced when the young doctor had to back out.

"He *had* to marry another girl. It was very embarrassing for me. This was a disgrace in those days."

Maggie's courage and her ability to bounce back were the key factors in helping her overcome this personal tragedy and continue with her life and her career.

Several years later, while she was working in New York City, she had a phone call from the doctor. He had been inducted into the service and was being shipped overseas. He called Maggie from the dock. By this time he was in a very unhappy marriage and pleaded with Maggie to write to him. He told her that if she didn't agree to write to him that he was going to kill himself.

In Maggie's natural, but unconventional manner, she told him, "Well, give me your address and I'll send you a gun."

In 1936, when Herbert Mayes became editor of the popular women's magazine, Pictorial Review, he offered Maggie a job, as associate editor.

"My parents, especially my father was very upset about me taking that job, but he didn't pay me but $25.00 a week and I was writing 125 pages a month. My mother kept telling him that he should pay me more or I was going to leave, but he said, 'she won't leave me!'

Maggie had been in New York City just a little over a year when the Pictorial Review magazine folded, leaving her jobless. She didn't tell her family because she knew her father would want her to come home.

"It's awful when a magazine fails. It's just like somebody dying. The whole staff was in tears. I was snuffing up martinis to take the curse off of me, but it didn't work and I came down with the flu. It was snowing in New York and I felt just miserable and hadn't been able to find another job.

"My father called me early one Friday morning and when I answered the phone, he said, 'what are you doing at home?' I knew I was in trouble and would have to think fast. I told him that I was just about to leave for the office. He asked me, 'which office?' I told him the Pictorial Review, where else? Then he told me that he had just read in Time that Pictorial Review had folded. I knew I had been found out. My father wanted me to get on the next train and come home, so I knew I had to find another job and fast."

For the next three years, Maggie, worked for the Hearst Promotional Service as a copywriter. Even though she was successful as a copywriter, she was not happy and started looking around for a more rewarding position and landed a job as associate editor for Good Housekeeping magazine. She was again working for her old boss, Herbert Mayes, who was now the editor of Good Housekeeping.

Through the forties, Maggie continued to supplement her income with her writing. She was writing stories like, *Whisper of Spring,* Good Housekeeping, December, 1940; and *The First Formal,* Good Housekeeping, September, 1940. During World War II, when patriotism was at it's peak, Maggie was writing timely stories, *A Letter From Corporal Lynch,* Life Story, 1942; and *For Sale — At A Sacrifice,* Good Housekeeping, 1942.

When the war ended and paper was not so limited, Good Housekeeping started publishing 15,000 word novelettes. Maggie was always on the lookout for these stories, but since this was an unusual length and required special guidelines, many times she ended up writing them herself.

Many of these stories were adapted for television plays. At one time she had over 200 short stories in print, and any one of them would have worked as a series.

One of her stories, *The Life of Lucy Gallant,* Good Housekeeping, 1953, was made into a successful movie, *Lucy Gallant,* released by Paramount Studios.

"When I wrote this story, I thought it was a perfect idea for a musical comedy. It had all the elements. The young lovers and the middle age couple. The scenery would have been magnificent because of the fashion displays, but I could never sell it as a musical."

The story was based on the life of a woman, who was disappointed in love and came to a booming Oklahoma oil town and established a dress shop.

"I was always terrified that I would run into Miss Jackson, the woman whose life was depicted in the story. I saw her one night at the Plaza Hotel. She was in town on a buying trip. I hid because I didn't want her to see me."

Maggie was so enraged at the way the screenplay was written that when the movie premiered in New York City, she refused to go.

"The original story was so much better than the screenplay. It was years before I saw the movie. I was in Rome and when it came on with Italian sub-titles, I just couldn't resist that. They hired good people for the movie, Charlton Heston and Jane Wyman. I loved Thelma Ritter. I thought she was marvelous, but the screenplay could have been much better.''

Even though Maggie has written books, she considers herself to be a magazine writer.

''I'm proud to be a magazine writer. That's what I set out to do.''

One of her most popular children's books, *Ben Franklin Of Old Philadelphia*, Random House, 1952, is still in print and came out in paperback in 1981.

When Maggie was in the hospital for a check up, she received a publicity poster on the paperback edition and promptly tacked it up on the wall. Her young doctor came in and told her that he had read that book when he was a boy. Maggie laughed and told him that it was coming out in paperback, so he could buy it for his young son.

When this book first came out, Maggie had a fan club, made up of eleven-year-old girls, who attended an all girl's school in Nashville, Tennessee.

''Early in my career, Faith Baldwin told me that I should answer every letter I received. I took the advice and started writing these young fans. I sent along a fifty cent piece with each letter because it had Franklin's picture on it. Needless to say this fan club grew so fast that I had to abandon the idea of sending the half dollars. I was using up all of my royalties, but I continued to answer every letter I received.''

Maggie's writing continued to be popular throughout the conventional fifties. Favorites with women then were *Virginia's Madness*, Woman's Home Companion, December, 1952; and *An Open Letter To Mothers*, American Weekly, 1959.

During the turbulent sixties she wrote, *Anything Can Happen*, McCalls, November, 1961; and *Kindness*, Glamour, December, 1962.

Even with the demanding schedule as editor, deadlines and crisis, Maggie still had enough creative energy left over to pursue her own writing career. In the midst of the vast and sweeping changes that were taking place around her, she was always able to keep her finger on the pulse of the American woman and continued to crank out story after story that was timely and timeless.

"All I ever wanted to do was to read and write. I never confused my writing with literature. I wrote for one purpose, to entertain."

Through the years, Maggie has been involved with so many different writing projects that it's like uncovering the golden egg when you discover that she wrote crime books, *Traffic With Evil,* under the name of Avery Johns.

"Doubleday ordered that book for their crime series. They picked that name because it could be either a man or woman."

The Normal Man, a short story, appeared in Playboy magazine, under the name of William Masters, "simply because they wouldn't buy anything carrying a woman's name."

Mary Parrish was her maternal grandmother's name. "I never knew her. She died when my mother was born. I always liked that name and took it for several pieces. When my agent called and told me that Hallmark had bought several of my quotes, I was thrilled. I was anxious to know which quotes and felt proud that my name would be associated with Hallmark. All of the quotes were under the name of Mary Parrish."

When her boss, Herbert Mayes, bought the rights to Margaret Truman's book, which was completely unwritten and when Margaret didn't show any signs of writing the book, he assigned Maggie the task of writing the book for Margaret.

"At that time I was managing editor and really didn't have the time to write this book, and when I told my boss that I didn't have time he said, 'you'll make the time!' and of course, I did. Margaret was a marvelous girl. All the Truman's were. They were a very typical American family. When I started gathering material for the book, I followed Margaret everywhere for several weeks. She was a good gal. When I asked her what she wore on such and such occasion she couldn't remember. I had to go to the library and look at old copies of the newspapers to find out.

"Right in the middle of the book, Margaret went to Italy and came home deeply in love. By this time I had completed the book. She told me I would have to change the ending of the book. I told her very strongly, what do you mean I will have to change the ending! As far as I was concerned it was finished.

"The book turned out to be charming because it was Margaret. McGraw Hill published it in 1961 under the name, *Souvenir.*

"I adored the whole Truman family and spent the weekend in their home when Margaret was married."

There were many disappointments in Maggie's life as writer and editor. One of the most difficult to swallow was when she found the first translation of the story of Anne Frank and brought it to America and tried desperately to get her boss to publish it.

"I rushed home with this translation in my hot hands and told my editor that this was perfect for Good Housekeeping. He read it and said he wouldn't publish it even if they gave it to him. His reasoning was that he felt nobody was interested in the war or Jews. He was a Jew. I told him that this was not about Jews or the war. It was about people who had to live in close contact and secrecy and the way they rubbed against each other. It was about their personality. But he wouldn't publish it and I told him he was wrong, deadly wrong, but he had the final say."

Maggie shipped the translation over to Doubleday and the rest is history.

She felt that she was always fighting an uphill battle because she was a woman. In all of her years working in the women's magazines she was never able to realize her one big career goal. She was never top editor on any publication.

The day she learned that she had been passed over for the top editor's job, "because she was a woman," she knew it was time to move on.

Her keen sense of timing and the fact that she pays attention to her intuitive feelings and is not afraid of change or to accept new challenges was the key factor in her shifting her career emphasis from magazines to book publication.

At a time when most people would be gearing down, Maggie was stepping out to accept new challenges in a yet unexplored field.

"The day I found out that I had been passed over again for the job of top editor, I quit that very day and went to work as senior editor for Doubleday the next day."

As a book editor, Maggie always tried to work with as many Texas writers as possible. She was Liz Carpenter's editor for, *Ruffles and Flourishes*, Doubleday, 1970. She worked with Jane Gilmore Rushing on two of her novels, *Walnut Grove,* Doubleday, 1964; and *Against The Moon,* Doubleday, 1968; and Leon Hale's *Turn South At The Second Bridge,* Doubleday. There were many, many other Texas writers.

When Lady Bird Johnson was writing her book, *White House Diary*, Maggie came to Texas to work with her.

"Mrs. Johnson is a born writer. She wrote her book herself. She recorded everything that happened in her life for a period of about five years. With the help of Liz Carpenter and her original editor, Mrs. Johnson chose the material from these tapes to be used in her book.

"When I took over the project of helping her get the book finished, I moved to Austin and we worked at Mrs. Johnson's office. Sometimes when she had to be at the ranch in the hill country; we'd move our work up there."

Whether Maggie is writing or editing, her true personality as a dynamic, outspoken, highly intelligent woman is always evident. She is not easily swayed and stands firm, if she feels she has a valid cause to champion.

When *White House Diary* was finished, Maggie picked out a picture for the cover, but Mrs. Johnson refused to use the picture Maggie had chosen.

"I really wanted to use that picture of her. It's my favorite. We argued about it and I lost."

After the book came out Mrs. Johnson sent the picture to Maggie. The handwritten inscription at the bottom of the picture sums up the feelings of so many of Maggie's friends.

"To Maggie, Whose Talents and Friendship I Will Always Treasure."

In 1970 when Maggie took mandatory retirement from Doubleday, she moved over to Holt, Rinehart and Winston and worked on special assignments. After her tour of duty there she was back in the women's magazines again as fiction book editor for Ladies' Home Journal.

Her advice to the aspiring writer is to, "write when you need the money."

"If I had been wealthy I'm not sure I would have ever published anything. I would have written, but maybe just for my own enjoyment."

Her favorite writing has always been fiction. The novel. "Truth emerges from the novel."

"If I could write something that would help people enjoy what is in the earth, on the earth and around them. If I could help people open their eyes and look and listen and learn, then that would be worth killing myself for. Most people walk down the street and never look at anything. They usually spend their time brooding over some wrong that has been done them. This is a waste of time. People need to enjoy what's around them. Be aware of all of the good things that is theirs to enjoy. The earth — the sky — the buildings and mostly other people."

Whether ghosting for a successful national syndicated newspaper column, *A Matter Of Taste,* for New York interior designer, William Pahlmann, or writing crime books for Doubleday, *Traffic Of Evil;* or short stories, *Fifth Row Center,* Good Housekeeping, 1973, (Avery Johns); or writing under her own name, Maggie will always be remembered as a giant in her field.

Her "creative literature" conceived from the imagination has enabled her to cross over the boundaries of time and crank out story after story for the American woman. She has shared a sob, a moan, a laugh and a piercing scream, with her faithful audience.

If her work had to be judged in a court of law, because of the overwhelming evidence of years of hard work, creative energy; and the unrelenting courage and ability to change and accept new and challenging responsibilities, the verdict would be quick and unanimous. "WELL DONE" would be a good and true verdict.

They would confirm of the writer, that she has been a powerful woman, ahead of her time, highly intelligent and self motivated. They would agree that she has used her "gifts" wisely. This true Texan — who never forgot her roots, has accomplished what she set out to do.

TO INSPIRE — TO EDUCATE — TO ENTERTAIN.

9

Joan Lowery Nixon

"I have always felt like a writer. There comes a time when you may be able to say, now I'm a published writer, but either way, whether you're published or unpublished, if you're putting your thoughts down on paper, you are a writer."

One evening Joan Nixon's husband, Nick, came home from work carrying a box of Joan's favorite candy. Joan was delighted until she opened the box and found a handwritten note. Hurriedly she unfolded the note and after reading it, she burst into tears.

"This was Nick's way of breaking the news to me that we were moving. It wasn't the move I objected to so strongly, we'd moved before because of Nick's job, but it was the place."

The note inside the candy box read, ''you're going to love Corpus Christi, Texas!''

"To me, Texas was a place where people rode their horses in among the big cactus trees. A place out of a John Wayne movie. I couldn't see myself living there."

Reluctantly, Joan packed and headed for her new home in Texas. Just before they reached Corpus Christi they hit a rain storm, but as they drove upon the bridge heading into the city, the rain stopped.

This beautiful city of Corpus Christi appeared to have been

Joan Lowery Nixon

washed clean by the rain and stood gleaming against the backdrop of the blue-green ocean. A giant rainbow swept down from the heavens and seemed to hang over the entire city. This was a wonderful welcome for Joan and her family. She turned to Nick and said, "this is an omen! I'm going to love this place!"

Texas was to provide Joan with the inspiration and the challenges that would cause her to take up her pen and pursue a career as a professional writer.

The setting of Joan's early life was quite a contrast with the setting of this ocean front city in Texas. She was born in Los Angeles, California, and grew up in Los Angeles and Hollywood.

Joan's interest in writing was established when she was very young. Even before she could read or write she would make up small poems and get her mother to write them down for her.

"My mother was very encouraging in any type of creative endeavor that me or my two younger sisters were interested in. She knew that I was interested in writing so she encouraged me to write."

To help their children learn and enjoy the "blend of creativity and voluntaryism," her parents helped them build and perform a puppet show. The whole family got involved. Her father made the curtains out of some old velvet drapes while her mother sewed the costumes for the puppets.

"We performed at children's hospitals and orphanages. We went to the Mary Knoll home for Japanese children and even though these children couldn't speak English, this didn't hamper them from enjoying the antics of the puppets. We did the classic, Punch and Judy and Peter Rabbit. Things all children enjoy."

When Joan was seventeen, her father bought a Ford and they started receiving the Ford Times magazine. After reading several issues of the magazine, Joan decided to write an article about how she and her husband and their three children went traveling in their Ford.

"Of course, I wasn't married then, I was still in high school, but I just put myself in my mother's place and wrote about the things we did when we traveled."

Ford Times bought the article and sent Joan a nice check for her efforts.

After graduating from the University of Southern California with a B.A. degree in journalism, Joan couldn't find work in that field and took a job teaching kindergarten. In order to get her teaching credentials she enrolled in the California State College and attended classes at night.

Because of her teaching position one of her professors suggested that she write her term paper on the value of kindergarten and submit it to the California State Teacher's Journal. He told Joan that there wouldn't be any pay for the article, but a great deal of prestige if she had something published in the journal. After thinking it over Joan did write her term paper on this subject, but instead of submitting it to the journal, she sent it to Parent's magazine. She thought she would try for a little pay along with the prestige. Parent's magazine bought the article and Joan was pleased that she had made the right decision on a market.

Little by little Joan was moving into the world of the professional writer. Several years later when her husband was transferred to Billings, Montana, she joined the American Association of University Women and was delighted to learn that one of their study groups was involved in creative writing.

"The fact that everybody in this group was busy writing gave me more of an incentive to go ahead and write. I had sold a few things, but very sparsely. Even though I had not sold a great deal, I always felt like a writer. If you are meant to be a writer, you feel like a writer whether you have had anything published or not. There comes a time when you may be able to say, now I'm a published writer, but either way, published or unpublished, if you're putting your thoughts down on paper, you are a writer."

Since she had two preschoolers who required a great deal of attention it was hard for her to find ample time for writing until she devised a unique method of tending her children and completing her work. She pulled the play pen over by the typewriter, slipped her right shoe off and hung her leg over the railings of the play pen.

"This allowed me to be close to my daughter while I was typing my manuscripts. Maureen would play with my toes and pull herself up on my leg. As important as my writing was becoming to me, my family always came first."

While Joan was in Billings she wrote many non-fiction articles for American Home, Woman's Day and the baby magazines.

Each year Joan's interest in writing grew stronger, but as her family increased it wasn't always easy to fit writing into her busy schedule as she had once been able to do. But in 1961 something happened that altered the way Joan viewed her writing and set her on a course that would prove to be the most successful of her life.

This was the year she attended her first writer's conference.

"Dee Woods was organizing the Southwest Writer's Conference then and it was in Corpus. I really wanted to go, but because I had four small children at home, I didn't see how I could, but Nick insisted that I get a sitter for the children and go to the conference.

"I attended one of the workshops geared to writing for children even though at that time I wasn't the least bit interested in the children's market. But after hearing the two speakers, John Ciardi and Kay Warwick I found myself being charged up. Kay told about making an average of fifty-nine sales a month writing part-time. She was a librarian in Robstown.

"I was so charged up after this workshop that when I got home I told Nick that I was going to start writing again.''

Joan's excitement spilled over into a letter she was writing to her parents. She told them about the conference and about her decision to start writing again.

"About a week after I had written that letter, I received a telephone call from my mother. She was thrilled with my decision to write, but she said that with four children, two still preschoolers, that I would find it very difficult, but she had a partial solution to this problem. She said, 'let me hire a cleaning woman for you one day a week and while she's there tell her to watch the little ones primarily and clean the house secondly. Then you go back to your bedroom and write.' She told me that she would stake me to a cleaning woman for one year, then she was betting that I would be able to take over after that.''

Joan was grateful for her mother's encouragement and accepted her offer. She hired a woman to come in each Wednesday and while she was there, Joan shut herself in her bedroom and began writing. It wasn't long before she was selling to Teen, Scholastic and many of the little magazines for children.

"I could get so much done on Wednesday because I would think it all out ahead of time. I had so much stored away that sometimes I could hardly wait for Wednesday because it would be spilling out. The dialogue would be writing itself.

"Sometimes I'd write 8,000 to 9,000 words on Wednesday, then on Sunday, Nick would play with the kids while I typed the manuscripts and got them ready to mail. The creative part seem to always come on Wednesday."

Joan followed this schedule for six months, then she called her mother and told her that she could handle the writing herself, but her mother said, "no, I promised that I would help you for a year and that's what I'll do."

Since Joan's mother was a writer, she knew the urgency Joan felt about getting on with her work.

When Joan was living in Hollywood and attending the University of Southern California, her mother heard about a night class being taught at Hollywood High School by a woman who was writing and producing radio plays.

"My mother knew that I was interested in this and since I didn't drive at the time she offered to sign up for the class and go with me."

Because of this course, Joan's mother, Margaret Lowery, became so interested that she was the one who took advantage of what she learned from this class and began writing and selling radio scripts. She wrote for the dramatic programs, Dr. Christian, Armstrong Circle Theater, Skippy Hollywood Theater and many other shows.

Joan didn't sell any radio scripts, but this class did afford her an unusual opportunity to go into the editorial end of magazine publishing.

"A woman in this class was the associate editor for a fan magazine, The Hollywood Entertainer, and she hired me as her assistant editor. This was an interesting and enjoyable job because I did in-depth interviews with some of the movie stars.

"One of my best interviews was with Cyd Charise. Unfortunately, before I really got my feet on the ground with the magazine it went broke, but I did enjoy the job while it lasted."

When Joan was twelve her family moved from Los Angeles to Hollywood.

"Most of the movie stars lived in Beverly Hills or Malibu, but we did have a couple of famous people living near us. Cecile B. DeMille and W. C. Fields lived just a few blocks away. Mr.

DeMille was our block warden during the war. I met him a few times and really liked him. He was such a gentleman. When he would see me walking home from school in the afternoon, he would tip his hat. This gesture made me feel like such a lady.''

When Joan was attending Hollywood High School, she was greatly influenced and encouraged to go into journalism by her English teacher, Bertha Standfast.

"I made sure that I was in Mrs. Standfast's class every year that I was in high school. I just loved that woman. She kept saying, 'you are going to be a writer.' At that time I didn't think of writing as a career. I was planning to go into the teaching profession, but Mrs. Standfast said, 'no, major in journalism at the university because you are going to be a writer.' I'm glad now that I took her advice.''

During that year of intense writing, while her mother was staking her to a cleaning woman, Joan decided to try her hand at writing a book for children. When she told her family that she was going to write a book, her two oldest daughters, Kathy and Maureen, insisted that she write a mystery and put them in it.

"Soon after I started thinking about writing this book, we went through our first hurricane. Hurricane Carla. I decided to use the hurricane in my story and did as my daughters had suggested. The book was a mystery and I used them as my main characters.

"When I finished the book I started sending it around like I had done with my short stories and articles. It went out twelve times and came home twelve times. Maybe I should have been discouraged, but I wasn't. I had gotten some very screwy rejection letters with some of my stories and had already learned to put these rejections in their proper place, so when my book manuscript came back, I just packed it up and shipped it off again.

"I remember getting one rejection letter, in the form of a check-list. The editor had checked the column saying that the characterizations are flat and uninteresting. I thought the story was good, but after I received this letter I was in a quandary wondering what I should do with this manuscript. Finally I decided to just stuff it into another envelope and try another publisher.

"This time the story sold. The editor who bought the story said that the characterizations were the strongest part of the story.

"After that, I resolved to take the attitude that unless the editor made specific suggestions about changing the manuscript to fit their requirements for publication that I was going to believe in my story and leave it the way it was written."

Joan continued looking for a publisher and when she learned that Criterion was wanting quality mysteries with interesting backgrounds, she sent them her manuscript. A few weeks later she received a letter from the editor saying he wanted to publish the book.

"This particular day, my husband, Nick, was home with a bad case of the flu. He was feeling just miserable. When I opened the letter from Criterion I was so excited and wanted to share some of this excitement with Nick and rushed into the bedroom waving the letter in front of his face. He was so sick that he could hardly raise his head off the pillow. All he could do was utter a painful grunt."

On the heels of this news, Joan received more exciting news the very next day. She had entered a local contest sponsored by Nolan's Po-Boy Sandwich Shop and the first prize was a trip for two to Mexico City. When she was notified that she had won the trip, she was anxious to tell Nick and rushed into the bedroom with her good news. Nick was still very ill with the flu.

"All he could do was grunt — umm. I still remind him that two of the most exciting moments of my life, which I wanted to share with him, had been quenched a bit by his half-smile and weak grunt."

Mystery of Hurricane Castle was published by Criterion in 1964 and launched Joan on a long and successful career in the children's book field. Each year, for the next five years, she wrote and published a mystery for Criterion.

Mystery of the Grinning Idol, 1965, *Mystery of the Hidden Cockatoo,* 1966, *Mystery of the Haunted Woods,* 1967, *Mystery of the Secret Stowaway,* 1968, and *Delbert the Plainclothes Detective,* 1971.

When Joan's husband was transferred to Houston in 1967, she did not consider the move a threat to her career, but accepted the move as a new challenge that would afford her greater opportunities to stretch and grow.

After the children were settled in their new school and when the curtain rods were bought and the house was in order, Joan began accepting speaking engagements from school groups and civic organizations and started teaching a creative writing class.

Like the designs in a kalaidoscope, Joan's writing was beginning to show significant changes, and her lively, inventive style was to thrust her into many different writing endeavors.

During this busy period while accepting outside speaking engagements, tending her family and keeping up with her books sales and writing new manuscripts, Joan developed a newspaper column and sold it to the *Houston Post.*

"The subject of the column was to take a look at the things that happen in a woman's life and see the funny side of it. The column ran for seven years, then I just simply didn't have time to do the column because I was so busy with my other writing projects."

As the years passed, Joan was becoming more and more interested in writing for the younger child. She wrote and sold many picture books. Among the most popular were, *Gloria-Chipmunk, Star!* Clarion, *Danger In Dinosaur Valley,* Putnam, and *Before You Were Born,* OSV Publisher.

One of her picture books, *Alligator Under The Bed,* Putnam, won the Texas Institute of Letters Award for the best children's book in 1975.

That same year her book, *Mysterious Red Tape Gang,* Putnam, won an Oscar's Scroll, from the Mystery Writer's of America. The winning of this scroll was to be the stepping stone that would lead Joan into a long association with this group.

"The year I won the Scroll was the first year that I had ever attended the Mystery Writer's awards banquet. That year the banquet was held in New York City. I was just enraptured because I was surrounded by so many writers, whose books I had been reading for years. I couldn't believe my good fortune at being able to actually meet and talk to these people. I was beginning to feel like a groupie!''

Later, as Joan became more active in this group, she served as one of the judges, selecting books for awards, in the children's mystery category.

"The books to be judged come from the publishers. When the judges get the new books they read and evaluate the book and send their report back to the chairman. I served as a judge for four years and during that time I read between 60 to 80 books a year. At times this was a chore, but it was also very exciting because I got to read so many new books.''

Because of her association with this group, Joan was invited to attend the first International Crime Writers Congress, hosted by the Crime Writers in Great Britain.

"Mystery writers from all over the world came to this meeting. One of the most interesting things, in addition to meeting and sharing ideas with the writers, was our visit to Scotland Yard. The Yard hosted a buffet for us and then took us on tour and showed us their museum. This was a special privilege since the museum is never opened to the general public. This was very interesting, but gruesome.''

In 1980, Joan's juvenile mystery, *The Kidnapping Of Christina Lattimore*, Harcourt, won the Edgar Award, given by the Mystery Writers of America; and her young adult novel, *The Seance*, Harcourt, won the Edgar Award in 1981.

Because of her writing, Joan has received many, many fan letters, and was especially touched by one written by a teen-age girl, who had read her book, *The Kidnapping of Christina Lattimore*. The girl told Joan that she was at a point where she didn't know what was important in her life. She didn't know where she was going and kept thinking about what Christina had said at the very end of the book. "I know now what's important. I am. It's a great feeling.''

"This book and especially these last lines had meant something to this girl. For her to write and share her feelings with me, as I had shared with her through my writing made me very happy.''

Joan takes her responsibility as a writer very seriously and believes that her readers deserve 100% of her talent and ability.

"I'm always amazed when people come up to me and say, 'so, you write for children! Isn't that sweet. When do you think you will be ready to write for adults?' This just infuriates me.

"Most people don't realize that you have to be more careful when you're writing for children than when you're writing for adults. Children are much, much more particular about what they read.

"When I was telling my son-in-law about these careless remarks that people make, he came up with a perfect answer for them.

"He said, 'tell these people that you're thinking about writing for adults about the same time your grandchildren's pediatrician decides that he's practiced on short people (kids) long enough, and now he's moving up to big people (adults).'

To put feet to her strong beliefs about giving children the very best in literature, Joan has served as board member of the International Board on Books for Young People. This group is interested in promoting reading around the world.

With her help, the Houston alumnae association of Kappa Delta has set up an essay contest for the Houston area high school seniors. The topic of the essay is, The Best Investment — A College Education, and cash prizes are awarded each year.

Joan is continuously stretching her writing ability and has been rewarded in many different ways for her efforts. Two of her non-fiction science books, co-authored with her husband, Hershell (Nick) Nixon, a geologist — *Glaciers, Nature's Frozen Rivers,* Dodd Mead, 1980, and *Volcanoes: Nature's Fireworks,* Dodd Mead, 1978 — were awarded certificates as outstanding science books by the National Science Teachers Association and the Children's Book Council Joint Committee.

Joan's expertise in writing mysteries was the subject of an article written for The Writer magazine. The response to the article was so good that Mr. Burack asked Joan if she would like to expand this article into a book. Joan was quick to say, "yes, I'll try."

Her efforts proved successful and her comprehensive book,

Writing Mysteries For Young People, was published by The Writer, Inc.

Joan's career has continued to soar since her reluctant move to Texas in 1961. Since that time she has written and sold over forty-eight books and has a half-dozen more under contract. Many of her books are reprinted in paperback and are selections of book clubs, such as Junior Literary Guild, Scholastic's Arrow and Lucky Books.

Joan has planted her roots deep in Texas and feels that Texas has afforded her a wonderful place to live and expand her talents. She is one of Texas' most prolific writers and will be remembered for her books and her work in the children's field.

10

Juanita Zachry

"I hope to always learn, to explore new horizons and to traverse many new plains of writing."

Shortly after Juanita turned seventeen she married B. A. Zachry and moved to Potosi, a farming community in West Texas, and started her married life as a farmer's wife. But this was not a foreign life for Juanita. She was raised on a farm and knew the pleasures and the pitfalls of making a living from the land.

As a young farm wife, Juanita learned to do everything in the field that a man could do. She operated machinery, plowed the fields, sowed the grain and drove the big tractors.

"In those early years of her marriage, the depression was just beginning to ease and we were trying to get a foothold and were determined that we wouldn't endure the hardships our parents had. We knew we would have to work hard to make a better life for ourselves, but we were willing to make the sacrifice."

In addition to her responsibilities in the field, Juanita kept a garden, canned, raised turkeys and cows and operated a small poultry farm. She sold her eggs boxed and graded and averaged 10¢ a dozen above the wholesale price.

During the busiest period of her life, while she was raising three children and tending to her duties on the farm, an old deep-seated dream pushed it's way back into her life and demanded a prominent place.

Juanita Zachry

"Ever since I had been a little girl, I had this secret dream that someday I would write stories and sell them. This dream never died. It was always very much a part of my life."

In those early years, Juanita knew that her writing wasn't good enough to sell, but she wanted it to be and began reading and studying the printed page, trying to learn the secrets they held.

One day while she was in Abilene she went to see Wendall Bedichek, the editor of the *Abilene Reporter News*. She asked him to give her a job as a stringer.

"My job as a stringer didn't last long. I wanted something more than this and went back to see Mr. Bedichek and convinced him that I could do feature stories if he would give me a chance and a by-line."

Juanita got the opportunity to write feature stories and was very conscientious about her work, but when her stories came out in the paper she was always disappointed.

"After those stories had been edited, the only thing I recognized was my by-line and the subject matter. I knew I had a lot more studying to do. I wasn't content working like this."

The only thing Juanita knew to do to improve her work was to compare her original stories to the published versions and try to find the missing elements. She pulled these stories apart, bit by bit, and soon was learning about leads, development and endings. As she incorporated some of the things she was learning into her own work, her writing began to improve and gradually her feature stories needed very little editing.

Since most of these stories were about friends, relatives or special events in the county, she was beginning to be recognized locally as a writer.

Her continued success with the newspaper gave her the courage to try writing for the magazines. She thought this would be a snap, since she had mastered the feature story, but she soon learned that there was a vast difference in writing for the newspaper and writing for the magazine market.

"When my stories came back, almost by return mail, I realized that I had a lot more studying to do. In those days I didn't know anyone else who was writing and I longed to find someone to help me. I heard about an elderly teacher, who had published several articles and was teaching at our rural school. I went to the school and followed her around, talking, asking questions, almost begging her to share her trade secrets with me. She practically ignored me."

In the past when Juanita had faced difficult decisions, she had always had to rely on herself. There were many times in her life when she felt that her back was "firmly against the wall." When there didn't seem to be a way out of her present situation, but she never lost hope. She refused to accept defeats. Her tremendous courage and her undying determination to succeed, to find a way, to accomplish her goals and ambitions had pulled her out of many troublesome situations and she knew that she would find a way to conquer this magazine market, as she had found ways to conquer her problems in the past.

When Juanita was fourteen, the great depression struck, and when it did, it changed her life completely. Her father was a prosperous cotton farmer, a leader in the community and a Baptist Deacon. Just prior to the depression he built a new eight room house for his family.

"We were the first family in the little farming community of Horn, to have an inside bathroom and kitchen cabinets. We were so proud of our new white house."

But as the country moved into the depression years, things began to change for Juanita and her family.

"We had never, never, stayed out of school for any reason. Papa was a trustee on the school board and felt that school was very important, but when the depression hit, we were not able to start to school because we had to stay home and pick the cotton. There wasn't enough money to pay the hired hands. I just couldn't believe this was happening to us. We had never encountered such financial problems before."

School had always been a special challenge for Juanita. She started when she was five and had stayed two grades ahead of her age level. When she was not able to return to school by Christmas, she was worried and asked her father when they could go back to school.

"Papa said, 'later, you'll go back to school, later.'

Juanita just couldn't accept this and after Christmas she confronted her father again about returning to school.

"Papa looked away from me, out across the cotton fields. There had only been a few bails gathered on over a hundred acres. The Jack Frost had stripped the fields bare. As Papa looked out across those dark and barren fields, his voice was just a whisper, 'I don't know, honey. I just don't know when you can go back.'

But Juanita knew that her father felt that they were not going to be able to go to school at all that year. Right then, she made up her mind to find a way to return to school.

"I knew I didn't want to go through life with a ninth grade education. Even if it meant walking the four miles to school, in the bitter cold, I was determined to do it. I was going to school."

Juanita's strong determination and her courage made it possible for her to get up that first cold winter morning, bundle up and strike out for the big consolidated school, some four miles away, in the neighboring community of Noodle.

She had to walk across a frozen wooded area, then along a busy, well traveled highway. As she walked toward the school, she could see a gin stack jetting up against the bleak sky. She knew the gin stack was near the school and set her sights on that distant mark.

But once she had reached her destination, her ordeal was not over. She was faced with the same four mile trek home in the afternoon. Her daily trip was eight miles in freezing weather. She soon realized that she couldn't continue going to school under these circumstances.

One afternoon it was so cold that Juanita knew she wouldn't be able to get home. She went by the constable's house and asked his wife if she could spend the night there, so she could go back to school the next day. The constable's wife allowed her to stay the night.

The next afternoon Juanita went back to the constable's house. This time she asked his wife if she could stay with them and work for her room and board so she could stay in school.

"Papa was against this. He had come from a long line of slave owners and said he couldn't bare the thought of one of his children hiring out as a servant. But I didn't consider myself to be a servant. I was doing honest work, something I knew I could do to put myself through school.''

Those were difficult years for Juanita. She lived at the constable's house and worked for her room and board during the winter months, but in the spring she returned home and walked the distance to school each day.

She was sixteen when she graduated from high school and wanted to go on to college, but lack of funds and the continuing economic state of the country forced her to compromise, and she enrolled in the National Business College in Abilene, again working to put herself through.

While she was in Abilene she met her future husband, B. A. Zachry and married him shortly after she finished her business course.

Through the years, Juanita had developed a sound philosophy, one she relied on again and again. This philosophy kept her from throwing in the towel when things really got rough.

''Always in the past when the chips were down, I had to rely on myself. Whether it was getting an education or making it as a writer. My philosophy has always been, I'll Find A Way Or Make One, to accomplish my goals and ambitions.''

When her magazine articles continued to be rejected, Juanita started an extensive study of about a half dozen of the farm magazines. When she felt she knew the market well enough, she submitted a filler to Farm & Ranch for their unusual animal column.

''My neighbor raised rabbits and shipped their furs up north. He had trained this big black cat to work just like a watch dog. It was really unusual seeing this big black cat minding those rabbits.''

Farm & Ranch bought the filler for $2.00. This was really a taste of victory to see her name and her article in a magazine.

''My family was always very supportive of my writing. They were always thrilled with my success no matter how small. My husband was my very best critic. He wasn't a writer, but he was an avid reader and had a scholar's mind. Often, he would read my stories and say, 'this won't sell,' then he would tell me why.

Other times he would say, 'this is good. It will sell.' He was usually right. I valued his judgment.''

Other members of Juanita's family recognized her talent and took a special interest in her work. Her brother-in-law, Roscoe Vinson, came out to the farm and told Juanita that if she was ever going to make it writing, she needed a good typewriter. He told her to go into town, find a typewriter and he would pay for it. He told her he expected her to repay him from the profits of her writing.

"I took Roscoe up on his offer and went to town and bought an Underwood typewriter for $45.00. Then I knew I had to make a success of writing to clear this debt.''

Juanita was always on the lookout for story ideas. One day she heard some ladies talking about how their old school had been converted into a community center.

"This was new and exciting and had never been done before in our area. I thought this was a story that needed to be told.''

She didn't waste any time going after the story and believed in this project so strongly that she was willing to invest not only her time, but her money. She hired a photographer, Boyd Graham, and agreed to pay him $1.00 for each picture.

"The night we were to go to the center, we dropped our three little ones off at my parent's house. My husband was always good about going with me and helping anyway he could. That night was really a gala affair. They held a special square dance just to help make the story a success.''

A few days later, the story, *Party Time At Pleasant Hill*, was finished and mailed to Farm & Ranch magazine with six pictures. They bought the article for $16.00.

"This was really a lot of money in 1948. I thought I had hit a gold mine.''

This was just the beginning of Juanita's sales to the farm magazines. She had sold over thirty articles when someone sent her a copy of the Writer's Digest magazine.

"After reading the articles on narrative techniques, hooks and themes in this amazing magazine, I realized how little I really knew about writing. I couldn't even recognize these essentials in my articles. But I wanted to learn and enrolled in the Writer's Digest School. It was difficult finding the extra time for this course. I had a hard enough time trying to sandwich in enough time for my writing projects. With the children, the chores on the farm and my garden, there just wasn't much time left. Sometimes I didn't have more than thirty minutes a day for my writing, but I waited eagerly for that time and taught myself to withdraw my mind from the chores and the everyday problems and really put all of my thoughts and energy into my work.

"There were times when I would be so discouraged, especially when an assignment came back all marked up. I'd say that my books and typewriter were for sale. The children would laugh and say, 'Mother will have that typewriter right back out again soon,' and of course, I did. I finished that course in about a year and really learned a lot."

In 1952, because of financial reasons, Juanita took a full time job in the county clerk's office and worked there for the next eight years.

"I used to take my lunch to work and eat in about fifteen minutes and spend the rest of my lunch hour writing. I was doing a lot of crossword puzzles then. There were times when I couldn't write at all, but I knew that one day I would be able to go back to it. When my youngest daughter finished college, I said I was going home and take the cover off my typewriter again and I did. This was when I really began to progress because I was able to be more consistent."

All of these years, while she was writing, Juanita was searching for someone to share her writing with and when she heard about a writer's group in Abilene she was eager to get involved with them.

"Since I didn't have a degree, I was only able to attend this group as an associate member and since the people were so unfriendly and discouraging, I decided it wasn't worth the effort, since I had to drive fifteen miles one way to attend the meetings. One of my deepest desires was to find a group and be able to share with them. I was so disappointed about this group."

Juanita was always trying to improve her writing and enrolled in the Famous Writer's Correspondence Course and later took an English course from the University of Oklahoma.

"I hope to always learn, to explore new horizons and to traverse many new plains of writing."

Juanita's struggle and her determination to succeed paid off and she has sold over 250 articles and short stories to local, regional and national markets.

From 1977 to 79, she was contributing editor for National Doll World magazine.

One of her favorite articles was on Clement Moore's classic, *A Visit From Saint Nicholas (The Night Before Christmas).*

"I have made an extensive study of Clement Moore and have a fairly large collection of his books. I have a copy of the original poem, *A Visit From Saint Nicholas*, when it was first printed in 1838. I have used this material along with a slide presentation for several television shows."

Juanita's favorite short story, *The Black Velvet Hat,* was published in the November 1976 issue of Home Life magazine. This fiction story is based on a memory.

"My mother was not an extravagant person, never, but when we went to town on our semi-annual shopping trip, Mama said that she needed a new hat. She didn't have a real nice dress and she wore cotton hose, but she was determined to have a new hat.

"Mama found this black velvet hat, with a wide brim and a great shimmering rose on the front. I think the clerk was just as amazed as we children were as we watched Mama try on that hat. She looked beautiful and turned to the clerk and said. 'I'll take it,' just as if she was used to buying hats like this.

"Even though Mama had to wear that hat with her cotton dress and cotton hose, she wore it with elegance and pride. She always said that we needed a few bright things in life to help us endure the difficult times."

Juanita was very busy writing her articles and short stories and had never given much thought to writing books, but when Ethel Boles and Maxine Hollingshead approached her about writing a book on the history of their community, she accepted the challenge and wrote, *Potosi, The First Hundred Years, 1867-1973.*

"Ethel and Maxine helped me with the book, Maxine was a great history buff and Ethel was good with promotion. The book sold well and is still selling. It's in it's second printing.''

After this book came out, Juanita was commissioned by a group of doctors to write, *This Man David, A Southern Planter*, 1971, Quality Publishers.

Another book which she was asked to do, *Forgotten Hero*, is the story of Calvin Graham, who joined the Navy when he was twelve and served fifteen months before he was discharged. This book was being considered by Lorimar for a possible television series.

''They kept the script for several months, but finally declined to bid on it as a weekly show. They said the production cost to recreate the battleship scenes were prohibitive.''

Early in her writing life, Juanita realized the need to share her experiences with someone, but she was never able to find even one person who had the common interest of writing. But she never gave up hope and knew that one day she would find those struggling, beginning writers and promised herself that she would share the things she had learned about writing with them. But she realized that in order to help others avoid the pitfalls and lessen the struggle to see their work in print, that she must first achieve some measure of success. This was one of the strong forces that kept her plugging away at writing.

As the years slipped by, Juanita began to meet a few people who were interested in writing.

''Most of these people were floundering about, uncertain, not really knowing what to do or how to do it. I knew it was time to organize a group.''

In 1969, Juanita invited a group of writers to meet with her in her home to talk about organizing the Abilene Writer's Guild. Twelve people showed up for that first meeting and the group grew so rapidly that within a few months they had outgrown meeting in homes and began meeting in the community room of the Savings and Loan.

After this group had been organized only about a year, they undertook the dynamic task of sponsoring a two-day Writer's Conference at Hardin-Simmons University.

The Guild is in it's 13th year and is very much a part of the Cultural Arts of Abilene.

To help encourage and strengthen the group, Juanita began teaching a creative writing class and later taught at the Abilene Fine Arts.

"There are rank beginners and people with masters degrees in my classes. Regardless of educational status, or lack of it, all of my students are striving for the same goal. To learn to write professionally. They want to learn and I've done my best to teach them what I wish someone had taught me thirty years ago."

But while she was teaching and working with the Guild, Juanita never let her own work suffer. She continued writing, producing both for the magazines and writing books.

Her book, *A History of Rural Taylor County,* was published by Eakin Publications in 1980.

Because of her husband's involvement in the Masons, Juanita was commissioned to do a book commemorating the 100th anniversary of the Abilene Masonic Lodge #559.

"To my knowledge I am the only woman who has ever written a masonic book. A committee of ten men researched the one hundred year history of their club and brought the material to me, since I wasn't permitted to see the minutes."

Before she finished this book, her husband learned he had cancer.

"We were told about the cancer on Christmas Eve of 1979. B. A. was gravely ill and we thought that he wouldn't leave the hospital, but he did and came home and thankfully he went into remission.

"We traveled and enjoyed our life together for the next few months and then in October 1980 he became weaker and was confined to home. He died the following April 21, 1981.

"In all of our 46 years of married life he never complained about me taking too much time with my writing or that I was burning too much gasoline. I'm surprised that he didn't since I failed so often, but he was always very supportive of my work."

After their children were grown they sold their farm and moved to Abilene, but Juanita always loved the country and considers herself to be a rural American. She has left her mark on this "big country" where she has lived and worked all of her life. She has spent most of her life writing about the people, their struggles and their victories in settling this land.

The last few paragraphs, in part, of her book, *Potosi, The First Hundred Years,* sums up her feelings for this magnificent country which she calls home.

"As we view the magnitude of the valley at sunset, we wonder what must have been visible to the observer one hundred years ago. Was the view serene and comforting to the ones who looked upon it as home? Would others follow here to make their homes in the great west.

"The first settlers prepared for us a rich heritage. As we view the landscape, beyond it's ready-made potential, a surge of joy and gladness and appreciation sweeps over us, finally we quote, *'This Land is my Land.'* "

11

Phyllis S. Prokop

"I am a writer. That's what I know myself to be. The fact that I have made this mental decision has helped me and has encouraged me to write constantly."

Phyllis Prokop has been writing most of her life. When she was a young girl, living on a farm in Weleetka, Oklahoma, she was constantly making lists of beautiful, descriptive words and expressions which she felt captured some emotion. As a young wife and mother, she was busy writing newspaper columns as she gradually moved into the book field.

It was only after she was working on her master's degree at the University of Houston, and discovered the modern poet, Wallace Stevens, who spoke of imagination and writing bringing order to life, that she began to understand why she had always had this strong compulsion to write.

"I realized that this is exactly what writing has always been for me — a source of order in my life. For as along as I can remember, I have been gathering together thoughts, ideas and words and by pulling these scattered thoughts together in a cohesive manner, I receive a particular joy and a sense of peace."

As a child, Phyllis had a great deal of leisure time and describes her childhood as, "thoughtful."

"My mother was an amateur psychologist and her theory was that if she never forced her children to work, they would grow up to love work. We lived on a busy farm, but my mother wanted us to be "ladies" and didn't permit us to have any con-

Phyllis S. Prokop

nection whatsoever with the farm work. We grew up doing absolutely nothing, except reading and studying. Mother felt this was enough for us to do. From the writing point of view, I think her philosophy gave me something very practical as she gifted me with whole seasons of free time. Summers were one long reading, walking, talking and thinking session.''

On rainy Saturdays, her mother would spend the entire day reading to her daughters, as they lay on a pallet, deeply absorbed in the stories.

''When she read, she took into herself the characters of the book and this made them seem so real to us.''

Her father was a storyteller and delighted in telling stories about storms, tornadoes and his early life experiences. He had been orphaned very young and had spent his youth going from ranch to ranch working as a cowboy.

''Daddy would become so involved in his stories that his eyes would tear up as he relived some of his past experiences.''

Because of her lifestyle and the abundance of time she had to spend on her studies, Phyllis was always a straight A student and graduated valedictorian of her high school class.

Shortly after graduation she enrolled in the University of Oklahoma and started working on a B.A. degree in Modern Languages. While she was at the university, she started writing articles, essays, comments and poetry. Later, she sold her poetry regularly to the poetry journals, the Baptist Student and The Teacher magazines.

She met her husband, Charles Prokop, at the university and they were married shortly before she graduated.

''These were the war years. Charles was an Ensign in the Navy and was on a new destroyer that made its shakedown cruise coming from the east coast and putting in at Mobile, Alabama. I met him in Mobile and we were married there. I took my final exams on my honeymoon.''

Shortly after they were married, Charles was shipped overseas and during the first two years of their marriage, they were together only six weeks.

When Charles came home and was discharged from the

Navy, he took a job with Exxon and they moved to Houston, Texas.

Through the years, Phyllis' strong desire to write was always evident. While her children were growing up she wrote a newspaper column, *Wisdom From The Word*, for the *Broken Arrow Ledger*, a newspaper in Oklahoma.

"On Monday mornings, after I got the children off to school, I would sit down and write the column. All week, I would be thinking about my subject and would be gathering material and making lists, as I have always done. By the time Monday came around, I usually had enough material to write the column."

After she finished the column, she turned her attention to her other writing. "I have always been involved in several projects at the same time. While I was doing this column, I was working on my book, *Conversations With Giants*, and on a book about King Hezekiah of Judah.

"For a long time, I thought this was not a good way for a writer to work — to be splattered about so much, but I finally realized that this has some real advantages. When I get an idea on anything, I try to record that idea immediately, no matter what other projects I'm working on.

"I believe we should honor every idea that comes to us. If we let ideas filter through our minds and never record them, these ideas may eventually cease to come.

"I set up a lot of file folders and notebooks on different topics and when I find something pertaining to that topic, I tuck it away in that folder or record it in that notebook. It doesn't matter whether it's a word, a phrase or a half chapter. Then when I get ready to put my paramount attention on that particular book or article a lot of the work is already done."

This is the way Phyllis wrote her first book, *Conversations With Giants*, Concordia Press, 1964.

"When I read the Bible each day, I would write my response to whatever I was reading. I filled so many notebooks that finally this just worked itself into a book."

To some degree, she used this same method with some of her other books, *Conversations With Prophets*, Concordia,

1966, and *Sunday Dinner Cookbook,* Broadman Press, 1969.

Phyllis has always been a versatile writer and while she was writing these books she was writing a food column for Mature Living Magazine.

In 1968 she was writing a newspaper column of comments, *Frankly Feminine,* for the Sunday *Oklahoman.* One week she said: "Peering through the flap of the tent at the vacation campsite, the Liberal Arts Mama says, 'If that stream continues to rise, I will get very nervous.' The Engineering Papa answers, 'No, if that stream continues to rise, you will get very wet.' Nearly every family includes both points of view."

When her older son was at Rice University in Houston and her younger son was in high school, she went back to the university and started a slow movement toward earning a master's degree. There were several things that she was determined to find out: What makes writing real literature and what sets good writing apart from mere writing?

During this time she completed her first long piece of work, *Under Every Green Tree*, the story of the life of King Hezekiah of Judah. This was a 100,000 word adult novel which was later cut to 30,000 words and published as a young people's novel, *The Sword and the Sundial,* David C. Cook, 1981.

After she had attained her master's degree, she wanted to find an outlet for some of the information she had gained through her studies, but she didn't want to take a full time job because she felt she wouldn't have enough time or creative energy for her own writing projects.

Her alternative was to organize a writing class that she could teach at her convenience, and this is what she did. She ran an ad in the local newspapers which proved successful and she taught her first class for fifteen students in the living room of a friend, Jane Chenevert.

After this creative writing class ended, there was so much enthusiasm to continue that Phyllis immediately organized a second class. This time the classes were held at a local church.

After the second class ended, the group had gained so much and was so supportive of each other that they decided to form a writing club.

"After we'd been meeting informally for about a year, we decided that we needed a name and picked Authors Unlimited of Houston. We kept the by-laws simple. Show up! Neatness does not count! And our annual retreat must be held as near Paris as possible!"

The reasons for organizing the group were mutual support in the form of encouragement, constructive criticism and the sharing of publication information. "This has proved to be one of the happiest and most profitable associations of my life. As each member faces new challenges there is the assurance of total support and this generates the courage to attempt ventures which would seem overwhelming alone.

"Another thing we do in the writing group, which has really been great for us, is to work with each other on projects. We have all agreed that if a member has an idea for a project she can invite the group to come in on it, but the idea and the published work will always belong to the person who had the original idea. It must be done this way or when the book comes out it will be nobody's book and the author just will not emotionally be able to put as much effort into promoting the finished product. Also, most editors say that books by a single author seem to do better in the marketplace."

When she had the idea for her *Three Ingredient Cookbook,* she tossed the idea out to the group and invited their participation. Most were eager to come in and they began gathering recipes and worked on the book for about two years.

"Since I grew up without knowing how to do anything, I had a clear and open mind when it came to cooking. When we married, my husband knew how to cook well, but I didn't. When I started studying recipes, hoping to learn, I found that most recipes required ten or fifteen ingredients. With my level of expertise I had never even heard of some of the ingredients. I just rebelled. In the back of my mind I knew there had to be an easier way and I started developing my own method of cooking, using as few ingredients as possible.

"Through the years I had accumulated literally dozens of recipes which were my favorites and many had only three ingredients. I started with these and Authors Unlimited submitted their favorites. When we had enough material, we went to a beautiful old Victorian house in Galveston for a weekend where we put the final touches on the manuscript.

"That was our first retreat in Galveston, quite near Paris. After we'd put the manuscript together I started sending it out to possible publishers. Several editors expressed varying degrees of interest, but none offered to publish it. I had sent the manuscript to Broadman, since they'd publish some of my other books, but they returned it.

"I knew this was a book for a specific market and might take a little time to place, so I stuck it back in the closet until I decided on another publisher. Before I had time to send it out again my editor from Broadman called and asked me if I still had the cookbook. I told him that I did and he asked me to send it back and let him take another look. I bundled it up, all 600 pages, and sent it back and he accepted it immediately. I think an experience like this illustrates that the market is constantly changing and we need to be flexible."

After publication, *The Three Ingredient Cookbook,* went into a second printing in five weeks.

On October 23, 1981, the President's Advisors from Houston Baptist University, hosted an autographing and tasting party for Phyllis on campus at the Moody Library. They sent out over 700 invitations and had a tremendous turn out. The members of the President's Advisors along with the members of Authors Unlimited prepared recipes from the cookbook and served them at the party.

When her book, *How To Wake Up Singing,* Broadman, was published, Jacque Goettsche hosted a beautiful 500 guest autographing party at the River Oaks Country Club. "All through my career people have been so kind and wonderful to me. In addition to the response of friendship, anything you write about, whether you are dealing with fiction or fact, gives you tremendous new knowledge. Each time you write a sentence or explore a new area for future sentences you have made an increment to your own being.

"It has been incredible, as little as I have done, to have people respond to me in such an open way. They include me in their lives and feel that they know me from my writing.''

Phyllis co-authored the book, *Your Day-By-Day Heaven-scope,* with Chloris Johnson and Anita Parks, Broadman, 1979; and also co-authored the book, *A Kind Of Splendor,* Broadman, 1980, with Jacque Goettsche. This book takes a close look at fourteen outstanding women and explores their world and their views of life.

''The original idea for the book was Jacque's. She had traveled in the near East and mid-East a great deal and everywhere she went women voiced the same question, 'what are American women really like?' They seemed intrigued with this subject. Jacque felt this question suggested a book that needed to be written.

''Writing this book was a life changing experience for me. I learned so much about life from the women interviewed. Just to be a part of their lives for a brief time was an unforgettable experience.

''What we were trying to do in the book, and I hope we succeeded, was not to write an expose'; rather, we wanted these women to tell our readers what they had learned from specific life experiences. What was so amazing to me was the great number of thoughts and experiences which we have in common, even if the interviewee was First Lady, Mrs. Carter.

''Rosalynn Carter is a down-to-earth person, but after all, this was the White House. I am not a nervous or excitable person, but I had butterflies when we were waiting to go into her office. The whole feeling of being in this historic place, coming through all the clearance, and the simple fact that we were there to interview the First Lady of America was awe inspiring.

''But the thing that really struck me was that the instant we saw her we felt at home. She extended her hand and asked, 'Now which one is Jacque and which is Phyllis?' She ushered us into her office and busied herself about making us comfortable, asking if we would like to sit here or there, and should the tape recorder be placed on this table?

''I realized with this interview, as with the others, that these people are friends and with friends there is much to talk about. Friend to friend. Woman to woman. The women interviewed were happy to share their lives with us; they had a contribution of ideas to make.

"Another interviewee, Jane Wyatt, has been a part of all of our lives. She has appeared in movies and television from *Lost Horizons* to *Father Knows Best*. She is a part of everyone's household. She is so at ease that it makes you feel at ease to be around her. There was no barrier here, or with any of the women — Ida Luttrell, Dale Evans, Liz Carpenter, Ann Campbell — they were all tremendous to visit.

"After the interview was over, so many of these women told us that talking through their experiences had opened a door for them and had helped them understand why certain things had happened in their lives. We became convinced that most people would profit from writing an autobiography or at least talking his or her life story into a tape recorder. It's really amazing what we have stored away or hidden in our minds."

When Jacque and Phyllis started working on this project, they did not have a firm assignment from a publisher, but they had faith in the subject matter and were firmly convinced that this book needed to be written and that it would sell.

They both realized when they went into this venture that their abilities and approach to writing were different, but they were determined to use this to their advantage.

Jacque took care of all contacts and scheduling of interviews. She opened an office and hired two secretaries to do the typing and transcribing of tapes.

"This was an ideal set-up for writing; we had a lovely office and unlimited help from Sandy Benson and Pam McElwee, both of whom were devoted to the book. When it came down to actually writing the copy, I read the tape transcriptions and wrote the chapters. Then, Jacque and I talked them over and made changes before the final copy was typed.

"When we started this project, I told Jacque that most books were written on the back of envelopes, but she laughed and said that this one would be different. I have lots of good memories to treasure from this book."

A Kind Of Splendor was nominated for an Angel Award given by Religion in Media. This recognition is presented much like the Oscar Awards. The ceremonies are held in Hollywood and statues are presented to the winners.

"We were so pleased that our book was nominated. I went to Hollywood for the presentation and even though we didn't win a statue, we came away with honorable mention. This was exciting."

Phyllis has won many awards and honors for her work. The American Business Women's Association voted her Woman Of The Year in 1974, and she won the Golden Pen Award, novel category, at the Southwest Writers' Conference in 1978. She is a popular speaker and reviewer at many women's clubs and professional groups throughout the Houston area.

She has been Director and participant in three annual seminars sponsored by Authors Unlimited of Houston and has been Director of other writing workshops and inspirational retreats.

She had a challenging assignment when Broadman Press asked her to teach an in-house educational seminar for their staff in Nashville, Tennessee.

"This was very exciting for me. We discussed the creative process from a writer's point of view and talked about ways of capturing the readers' interest in an opening statement. Since this was a group of professional writers, I am sure I learned much more from them than they did from me. I was impressed again with all the lessons we learn from constant writing; writing itself remains the best teacher.

"Writing has always been a very rewarding career for me. I would never want to give it up. When I'm not writing, I get so lonely to write. Even over Christmas holidays when writing must be pushed aside, I just can't wait to get back to it.

"When a book comes out there is always a certain amount of promotional work to be done. For a few months you find yourself speaking and autographing regularly. I love this. I love meeting the people, but during those times I do miss the writing. After I spend a certain amount of time on the promotional work I just suddenly recognize that it is time to go back to the typewriter. This is an emotion common to most writers, I have heard others describe their reactions in almost the same words.

"I hear aspiring writers say that they can't find the time for writing. What I try to tell them, even as I tell myself, is that you have to make the time. I'm always juggling my schedule trying to make more time; it's not easy for anyone, but I believe there is much more time available to all of us once we get geared into the habit of writing.

"I think space in the writing business is the same thing as time. If you have a place to write, your own space, and have everything you need for your writing, the time seems to come—perhaps because you can utilize your time better.

"If you don't make a place to work there is a tendency to get discouraged and say, 'oh, where is all that stuff for my writing? Do I really have time to drag all that out? Weariness and frustration may result from thinking about so much required preparation. This frustration burns creative energy and vigor is squandered on mechanics rather than on production.

"My feeling is that if you are a writer you owe yourself the courtesy of a place to write, and I believe this kindness to yourself will pay off in the long run.

"Writing is eternally exciting to me, and I feel as John Paul Jones must have felt when he said, well, more or less,

I Have Not Yet Begun To Write."

Jane Gilmore Rushing

12

Jane G. Rushing

"Nearly all of the fiction I've written has sprouted out of my West Texas country background like mesquite out of a prairie pasture."

The average life of a novel is less than a year, unless it is bought and produced by the film industry and even then there is no guarantee that the novel will be around for more than a few months or possibly a year after the movie is released.

There are exceptions, of course. Occasionally something happens that causes a novel to bounce back and enjoy a second life. This happened to Jane's novel, *Walnut Grove*. Thirteen years after the first publication date, it was reprinted as a "Redbook Novel," whirling it back into the limelight once again.

Using a book as old as *Walnut Grove* and publishing it in full, instead of condensing it, was a first for Redbook and a gratifying experience for Jane.

"Redbook was featuring Texas in their Christmas issue and the editor contacted me to see if I had a suitable short story that she could use. I didn't have a short story, but I remembered a segment in *Walnut Grove* about a Christmas celebration which took place in a country school at the turn of the century. I asked my editor at Doubleday to send a copy of the novel to the Redbook editor to see if she could use the Christmas segment. I was delighted when I learned that Redbook intended to reprint the book in full."

As with *Walnut Grove,* most of Jane's novels are about the people who have lived, loved and worked under the wide skies of West Texas, a region resembling the area where she grew up.

The rocky creeks and the hills are as much a part of her stories as the characters.

Jane was born in a rural community near Pyron, Texas and grew up on a farm. All four of her grandparents were pioneers in this region and the stories they told about their experiences in helping settle the land influenced Jane greatly when she began to write historical fiction about this region.

As a young child, Jane had a great interest in books and started writing stories and poems shortly after she learned to read. "I always wanted to be a writer. I knew this even as a very young girl. Somehow I just felt the need to write. There was something inside of me that needed to be expressed this way."

Since Jane was an only child, she had ample time for her studies and excelled in school. At fifteen, when most students are just beginning their high school education, Jane was graduating and making plans to enter college. By the time she was eighteen she had already attained a B.A. degree in journalism from Texas Tech University. She started her graduate work immediately and earned an M.A. degree in English when she was nineteen.

After she graduated she worked as a reporter for the *Abilene Reporter News* for a year then she switched careers. She entered the teaching profession and taught high school and college English for the next ten years.

In 1956 when she went back to Texas Tech University to start working on a Ph.D. she met James Rushing, a professor at the University and they were married November 29, 1956.

After her marriage, Jane completed her degree work and earned a Ph.D. in English in 1957.

Although Jane did not actively pursue a career as a writer she never lost her desire to write and did write and submit a few short stories through the years.

"I had received a few letters from editors saying that my stories showed promise, but nothing more. When our son was about two, I decided to try my hand at writing a novel. I had an old typewriter that I let him play with while I worked on my book. He learned his ABC's pecking away at that old typewriter. He wrote his book while I wrote mine. I worked on this book for a few years, but I could never seem to get it finished.''

In 1961, Jane made a decision that took both courage and determination and propelled her toward a sure and swift career in writing.

''I was between jobs and really didn't know if I wanted to continue teaching. What I really wanted to do was to write. I wanted to write fiction. I had made little efforts, but had never worked hard at achieving success.

''I knew it was time to either make plans to be a writer or give up the idea of writing altogether. I made a five year plan which I knew would mean a great deal of hard work and study, but I was now ready to do everything possible to succeed in the writing business or give it up and go on to something else.''

After she made her five year plan, Jane wrote a short story, *Against the Moon,* and sent it out, with high hopes that it would sell, but it didn't.

Shortly after the story came back her husband learned of the Emily Clark Balch contest sponsored by the Virginia Quarterly Review and encouraged her to enter her short story in the contest.

''We really didn't know anything about this contest. My husband had seen the announcement on the bulletin board at the University and since my story hadn't sold he thought I should try for an award. I entered my story, but really didn't think anything would come of it.''

To her surprise the story placed second and was published in the Virginia Quarterly Review. The names of the winners were carried in the *New York Times* and because of this exposure Jane received several letters from book publishers asking if she was working on a book.

''I had been working on the novel, *Walnut Grove,* for several years, in between doing my graduate work and getting my Ph.D. By this time I was in the middle of the book, but didn't have a great deal of confidence in my ability to carry it through to the end.

''Those letters gave me the courage that I needed to go ahead and finish the book.

''I enjoyed writing this book because it was based on the

things my parents and particularly my father told me about the early days in West Texas. He came to the area when he was 3 years old and literally grew up with the region.

"After I finished the book I sent it to Doubleday and they bought it.

"Since this was my first attempt at writing a novel there was a great deal of reshaping and revising before the manuscript was ready to be published.

"I had never taken any creative writing courses and had so much to learn. I was grateful that I had the opportunity to work closely with the editor at Doubleday. By working through my own manuscript I feel that I learned much more than I could have by just taking a course."

Jane's fiction career was launched with the publication of her short story, *Against The Moon,* which was later expanded into a novel. This became her second novel which was published by Doubleday.

"This story grew out of a situation that I had always remembered vividly from childhood. The last illness of my great-grandmother, who lived with my grandparents in their farm home. As it became clear that she would die, relatives began coming in from all over Texas. A group of people, many of whom did not know each other very well, were brought together for a time in a state of almost suspended animation, except that people always are animated, and it is easy to imagine the sorts of things that might happen.

"This situation is admittedly less likely to occur nowadays than a generation ago. More old people go to rest homes; many people die in hospitals. Yet I know families right now very much like the one in my book."

After her second novel, *Against The Moon,* was published the editor of The Writer magazine commissioned Jane to write an article delving into the life and work of the regional writer. The article, *People and Place,* was published in the September 1969 issue and the information presented then is still just as relevant today.

Jane describes herself in this article as a regional writer. She says, "there is danger in accepting anybody's theory about society, even your own, and then looking for examples to prove it, because you can always find them, whatever the theory may be. If you start with the particular instead of the general — in other words, follow the classic advice to "write about what you know" — you have a better chance to make a truer statement about the world and the people in it, even though you may know only a little patch of earth and a scant handful of people.

"Write what you know, then, is the first rule for the regional writer, but along with that goes the first caution. Be sure you really know. Don't get so carried away with recognizing the characteristics of your region that you forget all the people in it are still individuals."

Once Jane made her five year plan and started working toward publication a whole new career unfolded for her. Her lifelong dream of writing fiction was now a reality. With each new book idea came new challenges and new excitement.

In 1972 Jane's historical novel, *Tamzen* was published by Doubleday and was followed by *Mary Dove*, in 1974, and *The Raincrow*, in 1977.

Mary Dove won the LeBaron R. Barker, Jr., Fiction Award and was published in paperback by Avon and in England by Hodder and Stroughton, under the title, *Shadow Of The Dove*.

In her article, *The Roots of a Novel,* published in the July 1975 issue of The Writer, Jane speaks candidly about her novel, *Mary Dove*.

"I do not offer *Mary Dove* as an example of the technically perfect novel. But I feel that any success it has with a reader can be attributed to my basic feeling for the land, and my concept of a young girl growing up so close to that land and so dependent upon it that she becomes almost an embodiment of its spirit.

"Essentially, *Mary Dove,* is a book about the simple joy of a relationship between mankind and uncorrupted nature, the necessity for companionship and love, and (third stage) the development of a society that in its complexity inevitably introduces a new element: sin, but not without hope. Hence, the ending of *Mary Dove* is not altogether an unhappy one."

In this article Jane also says that, "plot, characters, and setting, inextricably entwined, do not, obviously, produce an automatic masterpiece. But a novelist who recognizes his most fundamental relationship with his material and allows it to prevail will have a good means of preserving unity in his work and thus a reasonable chance of achieving the effect that he hopes for. And a writer willing to accept the ''given'' in his life will be rewarded by story ideas he can work with.''

Three of Jane's novels, *Walnut Grove, Mary Dove,* and *Against The Moon* have appeared as ''Redbook novels.''

Even though Jane has a good track record with six books and numerous articles to her credit, there have been a few setbacks. All of her writing has not gone smoothly. When she was writing *The Raincrow*, her plan was to write the story from the omniscient viewpoint, but after writing about 200 pages she realized that she was not on the right track. She switched to first person, singular viewpoint and used flashbacks to bring the past and present together, enabling her to have the main action of the story take place in a short span of time.

''When I started getting bored with the story, I knew that my reader would be bored. I knew I had to do something to put life into the story.''

Jane usually thinks through a project very thoroughly before she begins the actual writing. She admits to being very critical of her own work and says that she has one completed manuscript that she is not sure that she will ever try to market.

''I may get back to it and do some rewriting or I may decide that that was the one I shouldn't have tried to write in the first place. Time will be the judge on this one.''

Jane collects folklore and when she attended a writer's conference at the West Texas College in Cannon, Texas, she was delighted to meet J. Everitt Hailey.

''When I told him that I was interested in the history of that region he invited me to look through his private files of interviews with old-timers. The best thing that comes from attending a conference is the wonderful people you meet and the help and inspiration you get from them.''

One writer who has been an inspiration to Jane and has been a great influence is Eudora Welty.

''I haven't tried to write the way she does. I don't think I could, but I think I have been inspired to look for character interpretations and have a sharper eye for the inner actions of the characters and a new sense of places through reading her books.''

During the time Jane was working on her novel, *The Raincrow,* she was also collaborating with Kline A. Nall, an English Professor at Texas Tech University, on a history of the University.

Evolution Of A University, co-authored with Kline A. Nall, was published by Madrona Press, 1975.

Most of Jane's books have been published by Doubleday. Her relationship with this publisher has been a pleasant one.

"I have always signed a contract giving them the option on my next book. Some writers may not prefer to do this, but I have always been satisfied with the way Doubleday has handled my books.

"I usually prefer not to write under contract. I have a couple of times, but I really don't like to work this way because I like to feel free about what I'm writing. I'm not always sure how long it will take to complete a novel. So much depends on what else is happening while I'm writing the book.

"I was slowed down on *The Raincrow* because I was working on the history of Texas Tech. When I got so involved with the history, I just didn't move as fast on *The Raincrow* as I had intended and of course I was using the wrong technique which just wasn't working.

"I'm most interested in writing fiction and that's what I'm best in. I think that the beginning writer will get along better to just follow the age old advice of writing about what you know. Something that you know well or feel comfortable with so that the dialogue comes naturally and the whole rhythm of the writing fits into your way of life or the way of life that you understand well. Write about what you know.

"I have been writing most all of my life, though I was in my thirties before I achieved my life-long ambition of publishing fiction. Most of this writing has been done about the things I know, the people in and around the region where I grew up.

"Except for two years in East Tennessee — a place I would love to write about if I knew it well enough — I have always lived in West Texas. Both sets of my grandparents settled in the same community on the rolling plains, where I grew up. My parents have lived there most of their lives, and I often go back to visit.

My grandparents were among the first of the farming people in that area; the ranchers had come some twenty years earlier, while the buffalo hunters were still having a little trouble with the Indians. I am fascinated by the way history is compressed in my home region. I wrote something about that in *Walnut Grove* and mean to write more about it still.

"This is a wonderful, lonely, understated sort of country. As a child planning to become a writer, I used to go off in the pasture as far as I could and try to fit myself into situations to match the literary-sounding descriptions I liked. As far as the eye could see, there was no sign of human habitation. It was awfully hard to get located so as not to see at least a windmill sticking up somewhere. Sometimes there wasn't a sound except the singing of the July flies in the mesquite trees. I haven't half said how that country really is; I hope I can some day; I intend to keep trying."

13

Jeannette Clift George

"There should be an area of trust in your career — trusting the Lord. I believe God is not going to masquerade an opportunity for a masterpiece."

Most of Jeannette's time and energy throughout her early life was spent developing and planning for an acting career. She pushed everything back into a corner, always reserving acting as her number one priority.

Because of her hard work and perseverance she was able to realize many of her career goals. She worked off-Broadway and toured with the New York Shakespeare Company. She played several seasons of summer stock in the East, at the Playhouse In The Park in Philadelphia and at the Arena Stage in Washington.

She also developed and presented her own one woman show at the Grammercy Arts Theater in New York, at the Dallas Theater III and at many civic clubs and other organizations in cities around the country.

In her hometown of Houston, Texas, she was a member of the resident company of the internationally known Alley Theater.

She is the founder, writer and producer for the After Din-

Jeannette Clift George

ner Players, a Christian drama company which offers Bible-based plays for churches, schools and theaters throughout the nation.

With all that she has accomplished in her chosen field and with her ambition and drive to succeed and to be the best that she can be, it would appear that when she was offered the leading role in a major motion picture that she would have readily accepted this new challenge.

She was a seasoned actress who played the leading role in some very outstanding stage plays such as *The Prime Of Miss Jean Brodie,* and *Dear Liar.* It would seem almost second nature for her to accept the film offer with a great deal of enthusiasm, but Jeannette did not accept this offer with enthusiasm, instead she panicked.

"The reason I panicked was that I had not had any significant film experience and this was a major film. Everybody in the film was a star.

"I was scared for me that I might not be able to do it. Also I wasn't sure that the character that I was to play would hold her own in the film. It was also frightening because it's really difficult playing a living woman, one who would be with us on the set. I was really concerned about this."

In the film, *The Hiding Place,* produced by World Wide Pictures, Jeannette was to portray Corrie ten Boom, a Dutch lady who saved the lives of scores of Jews in her native Holland during the Nazi occupation.

"When I was first contacted about the film, I was offered the part of Katje. At that time they were looking for a star to play the part of Corrie. Julie Harris had already been cast for the part of Corrie's sister."

The role of Corrie became very difficult to fill. Each star actress who was contacted had a good reason for declining the roll.

One actress had a London run which couldn't be cancelled. One's agent wouldn't let the actress he represented work without makeup. Another actress was not physically able to play the part.

The staff had seen Jeannette work and became convinced that she was the ideal choice for the roll of Corrie and had been all along. When the staff representative approached Jeannette about playing the part of Corrie, some of her reluctance and fear was related to the fact that a roll like this, if she were able to come up to the level of the part, would change her life. She was not eager to have her life changed and become known as a "Christian actress."

"I was a Christian—delighted to have the eternal existence of being a Christian and I didn't question that I was an actress, but I didn't want to become that "stereotyped—separated unto religion actress." I was also ill at ease—and a bit fearful of losing my own identity in the greatness of Corrie's personality."

After praying about the roll and being encouraged by the staff and her husband, Jeannette accepted the challenge and the added burden of a four month's location assignment in England and Holland.

As she had predicted, the film changed her life drastically. "This film plunged me into a category which I was totally unprepared for. I went into the venture as an actress and came out a Christian personality."

The film's general release was in 1975, and it has since shown to large audiences in the United States, Canada, Australia and England.

For her outstanding work in the film, Jeannette was nominated for a Golden Apple Award by the Hollywood Women's Press Club. She was also nominated for the Golden Globe Award by the Hollywood Foreign Press Association and was nominated for the Most Promising Newcomer of 1977 by the British Academy of Arts and Sciences.

After the film was released Fleming H. Revell contacted Jeannette about doing a book. She accepted this challenge because writing was not a new venture for her. She had been writing and producing her plays for years.

"I should have been more concerned with the thought of writing a book than I was with accepting the roll of Corrie in the film. I didn't know how hard it was to write a book. The editor gave me a deadline. I missed the first deadline and several after that. I developed an ulcer because I had never missed deadlines before, but I just couldn't get this book written.

"What finally got me off dead center was when Ernie Owens told me that he knew a very fine writer who was willing to travel with me, do some taping, and write the book for me.

"That did it! I got busy and had the manuscript to him at the next agreed upon deadline. I did not want anyone else writing my book. I felt that was my job.

"When I started the book I wanted to write a magnificent book, as all writers should aspire to do, but when I realized that it was not going to be a magnificent book, not the first time out of the chute, and shoved my ego out of the way and stopped trying to write a superior book, the writing began to come. I had to settle, as most writers do, for my best — it wasn't magnificent, but hopefully not all that bad either."

Some Run With Feet Of Clay was published by Fleming H. Revell in 1978 and when the first 20,000 copies were sold, the publisher sent Jeannette a note saying, "wonderful."

Even though Jeannette had trouble making the deadlines on the book, this was the positive side of her performance in the movie, *The Hiding Place.*

There were some negative results. "To a degree, I lost a lot of my contact with the commercial theater, not so much professionally as socially. Because of the film I was now a known Christian. I was a known Christian before, but not KNOWN.

"After the film was released I was in rehearsal for a play at the Alley Theater in Houston and several apprentice actors and actresses came to watch my rehearsals. I was so flattered until I found out that they had heard that I was a "big haloed Christian" and they wanted to see what would happen when my "sanctified state" tried to blend with "the everyday rehearsals" of the company.

"I was told later that several of the apprentices had commented on the fact that I had worked well with the director. They were surprised and expected me to be different.

"I am different! But the difference does not mean that I don't react as a human being and the difference does not mean that I am not a worker."

Jeannette has always been a worker. Her life's plan has always centered around the acting and writing profession and she has worked hard to achieve and remain on a professional level.

She was an only child and grew up in Houston and San Angelo.

"I grew up in a loving family. I'm very grateful for that. My parents were happy for me to be involved in the theater until they realized that my intentions were something more than just playing around with it. They were deeply concerned when they realized that I was planning to make this a full time career."

After Jeannette graduated from Lamar High School in Houston, she entered Stephens College in Missouri and from there entered and completed her education at the University of Texas in Austin.

She admits being a very shy person and when she was younger she was very impressionable.

"While I was at Stephens College I was so impressionable that I think I would have taken on the form of any personality that affected me at that time.

"I stayed with a very gentle lady, Maude Adams, who loved theater and taught me so much. She was very strong on hard work, commitment, beauty and love.

"One thing she said that has always stayed with me and I think of it even after all of these years and try to apply it to my life. She said, something to this effect, never cause anyone to laugh at that which you hold dear."

Jeannette encourages young aspiring writers and actors to get a good general education, which she says usually upsets them, because this sounds like the same advice they get from their parents. She also encourages students who want to go into the arts to choose their school primarily for it's value in general education.

"After you get your general education there are places you can go to get a specialized education and learn needed skills.

"I regret that I was not aware of this when I was in school. My attitude toward higher education was to get it over with — everything I did — every class I took — every lecture I attended — everything was a means of just getting it over with so that I could do what I wanted to do — and that was to go to New York and act.

"Of course, now I realize that my education was in preparation for what I wanted to do, but I didn't realize that then and I was rebellious the whole time I was in school."

When Jeannette was at the University of Texas, one of her History Professors took her aside and asked her why she was in school. Her answer came quickly, "because I have to finish school before I can go to New York and do theater."

He asked her if she was interested in any of her studies. She said, "no, nothing I'm studying here will equip me for what I plan to do with my life."

This gentle man asked Jeannette what type of rolls she intended to play when she went to New York.

Jeannette took on her most superior characteristics and answered quite smugly, "I am primarily a classical actress — I intend to be involved in classical theater."

The Professor said, "if you were to play the roll of Queen Elizabeth, how would you play it?"

Feeling very well qualified Jeannette replied, "I would play her as the person she was rather than a stereotyped character."

When the Professor asked her how she would know what kind of person Queen Elizabeth was, Jeannette told him that she would study the script.

"What else would you study?" he asked.

"I would study about the way she lived. What she did."

The Professor looked her square in the eye and asked, "did it ever occur to you that that is what we do in this history class?"

Soon after she graduated from the University of Texas with a Bachelor of Fine Arts degree, she talked her best friend, Mary Jo Priddy, into going to New York with her.

"When we started talking about going to New York, Mary Jo assumed that we would fly, but I was just terrified at the thought of flying so I talked her into going by train. I told her that we would have a long layover in New Orleans and would find some wonderful, unique places and have a real good time.

"I was always quick to verbalize about accepting challenges and new adventures, but in reality when it came to carrying through, I would always pull back. We spent our time in New

Orleans in the depot because she couldn't budge me from that spot.

"She spent her time writing post cards telling our friends that if they came to New Orleans, not to miss the depot. "You'll love it," she wrote. "This is where we spent the first part of our venture."

Even though Jeannette had a great appetite to work in theater, it was very difficult for her in New York because she was so shy and was not very assertive. The management of the profession was not only foreign but frightening to her and she got most of the jobs in theater by flukes.

When she went to pick up one of her friends who was auditioning for a part in a company, Jeannette was mistaken for an actress who had come to audition. When they asked her to do a scene, she did.

"I was very at ease once I got on stage. I could handle myself more on the stage than I could one to one. I did the scene and was accepted in the company before they realized that I had not even applied.

"I did an off-Broadway show during that time. I worked at the airlines from midnight until 8 a.m. and then after a couple of hours of sleep, I was off interviewing. Later I was rehearsing or doing the play.

"I did some television commercials and a pilot for a series. I sold comet cleanser, aspirin and frozen food.

"My father had been upset about my acting career because he was worried that I couldn't support myself. When he realized that my acting was not just a whim and when he could see that I was supporting myself, he accepted my acting career and was pleased. When he passed away I flew home immediately and when a friend met me at the airport she told me that my father had seen one of my commercials the night before he died and was so excited."

Jeannette was working in theater in New York when she had an encounter with Christ.

"I believe that relationship with God clarified my identity. It gave me a person to be — ME. I think one of the things I was looking for in theater was a denial of identity. I was working out so many personal problems. Theater was a wonderful place to hide.

"This encounter with Christ and my new found identity caused me a great deal of trouble. I think one of the reasons I was able to accomplish what I had in theater was because I was easy to get along with. I never questioned anything.

"When I began to realize that I had more personal choices and began to learn to exercise those choices there was a difference in my attitude. I was beginning to suspect that there was a world outside the theater and that is very dangerous to the theater mind. Part of theater's dynamics is in believing that it's reality."

It was during this period in Jeannette's life, while she was a busy actress in New York, that she started writing monologues.

"I was trying to give communication to the identity I was claiming."

She began to perform some of the monologues and later did a one woman show. She describes the one woman show as, "a comedy — very corny — very sentimental — and very me!"

Jeannette was branching out in her writing. She wrote an act of short sketches on marriage. She did a collection of Dear Abby Letters. She did some adaptations and some children's theater. She was fast becoming a notable writer and actress.

When she was offered a job in the resident company at the Alley Theater in Houston she accepted. She kept her apartment in New York for about two years, alternating between jobs in Houston and New York, but finally she made the break from New York and made her homebase Houston.

She took a job in the performing arts department at Houston Baptist University and established the After Dinner Players, a drama group made up of students on campus.

"I came to Houston on full salary for the Alley. That was my full time job, but I still needed an outlet to share some of the things I was learning from the Bible. I was really concerned for the college drama student and I wanted to do some experimental theater. This was the main reason I took the job at the University.

"After I formed the After Dinner Players, I began looking for suitable scripts, but couldn't find any, so I started writing them myself. The company was first established from a very fragile initial plan. It never crossed my mind then that one day we would be where we are now — well established in our own Grace Theater — with an administrative staff and a full resident and traveling company. This was not my plan at all.''

When the university officials felt that the university could no longer support this experimental company, Jeannette saw no reason to stay on campus and decided to terminate her teaching involvement with the university. Her main interest was drama and she was not seeking a full time teaching position.

"We kept the company in a very loose organization. I was a little bit divided because I was still working full time at the Alley. My rehearsals with the A.D. Players had to be worked in and around my schedule.

"We were based in Nancy Smith's recreation room. She was a dear friend to let us store our things there. We worked anyplace we could. I started writing two and three plays a year. They all had a theme. The evening plays were made up into sections so that they could be booked separately.

"Then I began writing, 1, 2 and 3 act plays. We were doing a lot of short ten minute sequences and improvisations — which we don't do now.''

All of the plays had a Biblical reference. Her play, *Jonah*, is a delightful account of the story of the unwilling missionary. It runs twenty minutes.

Mary and Martha is the story of how Christ met these two sisters at the point of their need. (20 minutes).

The Thief Of The Cross is a dramatization of the last few minutes in the life of one of the thieves crucified with Christ. (10 minutes).

Jeannette has chosen unusual titles for some of her plays. "Since the Bible is the manuscript I have taken most of my titles from the standard proofreader's notations.''

Demi — Tasse — Et Cetera — Ex — Footnote — Memo — Item — Marginal Notes and *Ret* are just a few of more than thirty plays.

Jeannette transfers Bible truths, stories and characters into theatrical plays which move, enlighten and entertain grateful audiences.

For her writing for the A.D. Players, she was the recipient of the Matrix Award, an award given for outstanding contributions to the community. For her work with students of drama, she was initiated as an honorary member of Alpha Delta Kappa, an international teacher's sorority.

In 1976 she received the Sheild Award of Delta Gamma Fraternity for distinguised achievement through professional or volunteer services to the community.

After Jeannette moved back to Houston and was working full time at the Alley, she met Lorraine M. George and they were married August 14, 1971.

"I married late, but right on time for me. My husband is a wonderful, secure man who is not threatened by the tides of my success. He's very supportive and very encouraging."

In the early part of 1982, Jeannette played the part of Martha in Ragan Courtney's television play, *Bright New Wings.*

She is constantly on the go with her company and her numerous speaking engagements. Because Jeannette is such a shy person she has some difficulty in handling Jeannette Clift George, in a one on one situation, that she doesn't have when she steps onto the stage and assumes the roll of a character.

"I'm a utilitarian actress — give me a part to play and I'm fine, but sometimes in trying to handle Jeannette it's a degree of positive sham. Sometimes I have to just put Jeannette aside in order to satisfy the assignment."

Jeannette says that when she's doing what she wants to do and feels led to do, her energy level is just incredible.

"Energy has been a natural thing for me until the last few years. Now I reach down where it's supposed to be and it's not there and this just shocks me.

"I take that to mean, rather than aging, which is a natural factor, as a hint to check to see if my energy is being properly expended. Creative energy must be treasured.

"I've tried to teach myself not to react in horror to an empty space. That fleeting thought that this opportunity may never come again and make peace with it. That opportunity may never come again — SO — let it go.

"There should be an area of trust in your career — trusting the Lord. I believe God is not going to masquerade an opportunity for a masterpiece."

Jeannette Clift George — native Texan, accomplished actress, outstanding playwright, dedicated Bible teacher and a woman of great vision. Stepping out and moving forward in a changing world — knowing her limitations, but succeeding in spite of them.

14

Ethel Lindamood Evey

"My goal is to write books that are so absorbing, exciting and meaningful that the reader will fall in love with them and will want to read more."

When Ethel started researching old diaries and journals gathering information about her great-great-grandfather, William P. Bradshaw, to be included in a family history, she did not realize that this research would be instrumental in adding another dimension to her writing life. A deep interest in history was kindled and thrust Ethel into a long successful career writing historical fiction and non-fiction.

Her book, *Stowaway To Texas,* Larksdale Press, 1982, was a direct result of her searching through some old diaries and journals.

"When I came across an account of a young boy who was left stranded on a schooner bound for Texas when his father was taken off the ship for nonpayment of debts, I thought that this was a marvelous idea for a book.

"I first became interested in Texas history while I was doing the research on my great-great-grandfather who came to Texas in 1820 — one year before Stephen F. Austin brought his settlers. I found my grandfather's name in many of the diaries and journals of the men who wrote about Texas in the early days.

"I built this story with imaginary characters, but the events

Ethel L. Evey

which they are involved in are true. All of the places in the story are real places and most of them still exist today. The background material for this book came from diaries and journals of people who were in Texas in 1837 and who left vivid descriptions of the country and the people.''

Other ideas for stories were generated as Ethel plowed through the old diaries and journals which were stored in the Pasadena Public Library.

Her article, *That First San Jacinto Day,* written about the celebration of the first anniversary of the Battle of San Jacinto was first sold to Tempo magazine, the Sunday supplement of the *Houston Post* newspaper and the article was later restyled for *The Dallas Times Herald.*

As she began to dig deeper into Texas historical data, Ethel came up with, *The Campbells That Walked Miles For Uncle Sam,* Tempo and *Jeff Davis' Folly,* Scouting magazine.

Because Ethel had been an avid reader since childhood she found a great deal of enjoyment in these research projects.

''My father always read to us. He was the one who got me interested in reading. When I was a child I was always perfectly content to be off by myself reading a book. My father was a Baptist Minister and taught school in a small two room country schoolhouse. He believed that books were important and built a little room in the back of the schoolhouse and made a library. He filled one shelf with children's books. I read every book on that shelf.''

When Ethel was sixteen and living in Tyler, Texas and attending high school, she met John Lindamood who was working as a house painter. They fell in love, eloped and were married.

''John was fourteen years older than me and as you can imagine my parents were really upset.''

For the next twenty years Ethel's life was centered around her home and family. Her life with John ended in 1951 when he died of cancer. She was left with three children, no high school education and no means of supporting herself. It was hard, venturing out and seeking employment, but Ethel knew that she must find work and landed a job with an aircraft company. She worked there for about a year, then she sold her house, packed up and moved to Georgia, seeking a better way of life.

"The President of Taccoa Falls College in Georgia, came to our church recruiting for the college. This was a combination high school and college. You could get a high school certificate there and continue college work. This seemed like a great place for me to be so I just sold out, packed up and left."

Ethel got a job as housemother on campus and started her venture into higher education. She stayed on campus for two years until her oldest daughter, Nelda, graduated from high school. After Nelda was settled into a good job, Ethel took her two youngest children, Loretta, 10, and David, 14, and went to Hauck, Arizona to work as a Missionary in a non-denominational mission on a Navajo reservation.

They lived in the Mission building on the reservation and the children went to the reservation school. Ethel taught Bible classes at the Mission on Sunday and taught a weekly class at the reservation boarding school which was about ten miles away.

"We fed the Indians at noon on Sunday. Some of them came a great distance. Before I went there the Missionaries cooked a big pot of pinto beans and gave the Indians bread and coffee. When I started cooking, I put onions and tomatoes in the beans and always had some kind of dessert. Cupcakes or pumpkin pie on Thanksgiving. The Indians really liked that."

Ethel enjoyed her work on the reservation, but there were some sad experiences. Early one morning just before daybreak, an Indian couple brought their seriously ill two year old son to the Mission.

When Ethel saw the child she knew he was gravely ill and hurriedly bundled the baby in a warm blanket. After she had tucked the parents and child snugly into her car, she started what she knew was a frantic race with death.

"The hospital was thirty miles away. The baby's breathing was so labored — I knew it was touch and go. I flew over that road. When we reached the hospital the doctors and nurses did everything they could, but it was too late."

After the pronouncement of death, Ethel was faced with the task of driving the parents and baby back to the Mission.

"These Indians were Catholic — they didn't belong to our

Mission, but the Catholic Mission charged for burial in their cemetery, and we didn't, so we were faced with the baby's burial. The Navajo woman who stayed at the Mission with us assisted me in washing the baby's body and getting it ready for a Christian burial.

"I had never done anything like this before and it was really hard. One of the hardest things I have ever done. Some of the men made a burial box and we buried the baby in the Mission Cemetery."

Since her children were enrolled in the reservation school and the quality of education there was so poor, Ethel felt that she must leave the Mission so that her children could get a better education.

"I really liked being at the Mission. It was interesting and rewarding work, but the school David attended was terrible. The teacher drank and used so much profanity. He really had it in for the Navajo's and shouldn't have been teaching there."

Since her children's education was so important to her, she left the reservation and moved to Arlington, Texas and lived and worked there until her son, David, finished high school and went into the service.

After David went into the service, Ethel took her youngest daughter, Loretta, and returned to Taccoa Falls College. She worked as housemother for the next four years while Loretta finished high school.

In the mid-fifties Ethel began thinking seriously about writing as a part-time career. She had always wanted to write, but couldn't get anything down on paper. She began recounting some of her experiences while she was at the Mission in Arizona and decided to try writing a short story.

She wrote a story about an Indian boy, titled it, *Comanche Revenge*, and sold it the first time out to Council Fires magazine for $35.00. "I was on top of the world when I sold this story. I just knew I had made it as a writer. I quickly wrote more stories and sent them out, but to my surprise, they all came back. It didn't take me long to realize that there wasn't any room for amateurs in the competitive writing field. I knew that I needed to get some professional training and enrolled in the Newspaper

Institute of America, a correspondence course. Later I enrolled in the Benson Barrett course. Each of these courses was a tremendous help, but I learned to write by writing.''

It wasn't long before Ethel was selling some of her lesson assignments. Two of her children's stories which she had written for the Benson Barrett course sold. *Timmy's Trouble* sold to Wonder Time magazine and *Company Manners* sold to Three/Four magazine.

Through these courses Ethel was learning the proper way to write and the proper way to market her stories. She began to discover the age old adage of writing about ''what you know'' and began reaching back into her past searching for story ideas.

''My father used to tell us a story about a corn doll. I didn't remember many of the details of the story, but I always liked the story and decided to write my own version. I called my story, *Johnny And The Tattletale Doll*. I sold the story to My Sunday Reader.''

This story was about a boy and his twin sister. The boy received a ball made from twine for his birthday and his sister received a rag doll, stuffed with corn. The boy was pleased with his present and tried to persuade his sister to play ball with him, but she was preoccupied with her new doll and ignored him.

Wanting to tease his sister, the boy buried the doll behind the barn. He had intended to retrieve the doll later that day, but as fate would have it, before he could unearth the doll, it rained. He knew the doll would be ruined and pretended that he knew nothing about the doll's disappearance. Everyone thought the dog had dragged it off.

Several weeks later when the boy's father was behind the barn, he noticed small sprouts of corn growing in the shape of a rag doll. It didn't take him long to figure out what had happened, but the boys conscience was hurting so bad that he confessed before his father confronted him.

Another story, *A Red Ball of Yarn*, Adventure magazine, was based on a story Ethel's grandmother had told her. It was also a character building story.

Her adult short story, *The Perfect Birthday*, Lutheran

Women, was based on an anecdote. Ethel was beginning to learn to use every source to generate story ideas.

After her son's bout with pneumonia, she wrote an article about the accidental discovery of the "miracle drug" penicillin. This sold to Junior Life, 1969, and Words of Cheer, 1976.

After her youngest daughter finished high school at Taccoa Falls and entered Nursing School, Ethel came back to Texas to care for her mother. When Loretta finished Nurses' Training she landed a job at Bayshore Hospital in Pasadena, Texas, and Ethel moved there to be with her.

To help support herself she took a job in a fabric shop and as always was constantly searching for story ideas. She became curious about what raw materials were used in making synthetic materials and began an extensive research project with the thought of writing a book, *The Great Man-Made Fiber Spinout.*

When her daughter asked her what her book was about Ethel told her it was about polyester. Her daughter always enjoyed reading her mother's stories and became very excited.

"Polly Esther who?" she asked.

"Loretta was used to me writing about people. I'm just about finished with this book and I hope to have it in the marketplace soon."

In 1967 while doing research at the Pasadena Public Library, Ethel read a notice of a meeting of the Pasadena Writer's Club.

"I decided to go to a meeting and was so impressed with the group that I joined as soon as I was eligible. This was a wonderful group of writers. Sibyl Hancock, Iva Nell Elder and Jean Burns were members. They helped me a great deal. Joan Nixon came and taught a six weeks fiction course which was really a fine class. We all learned so much from her."

In 1972, after twenty years of widowhood, Ethel met Ed Evey and they were married a short time later.

"Ed was a retired contractor when we met, but he owned a small music publishing company, Edmark Productions, which he started as a hobby. He has produced several records — *Time,* by the Pozo Seco Singers was first released in 1966 and is still playing in the United States and several foreign countries. Don

Williams who was a member of that group, got his start from that record and has gone on to the top in the country western field.

"Since Ed is also a writer and in the record business, he knows some of the pleasures and pitfalls of the writing business. He's given me a great deal of support and several good ideas for stories.

"He was the one who suggested that I write a humorous tall-tale type book about Arizona. Since Ed suggested the book I thought it would be fun to name it, *Use Your Head Ed.* I haven't had time to think about a market yet, since I have been so busy promoting my Stowaway book, but I think it will sell."

Ethel has not had an easy life. There have been many struggles, but she says that through all of her struggles and frustrations in her writing life and her personal life that she has never gotten depressed.

"I'm not the worrying kind. I take things kind of easy. I've always trusted in God and have leaned upon Him to help me. He has never let me down. I always knew by trusting God things would work out—in my personal life as well as with my career."

Just after Ethel started writing her Stowaway book, she attended a seminar sponsored by the Associated Authors of Children's Literature, a Houston based writing group.

"Since I already had some of my book written, I decided to submit the first chapter for criticism. This was really a break for me because Johnny Bass took my chapter and really went over it thoroughly and gave me so much help. I will always be grateful to Johnny and that group for their encouragement. When I was asked to become a member of that group I was delighted and accepted immediately."

Since Ethel's first sale in 1958, she has not had many dry spells. Her writing has sold steadily. Her creative-informative Who-What-When-Why articles published in the Encyclopedia Britannica Learning Program have been a favorite with children.

"I'm naturally a curious person which, I suppose, accounts for my writing these articles. I wrote *What Makes a Jumping Bean Jump?* after a friend gave me a jumping bean. I thought that a child would enjoy knowing this."

Some of Ethel's other Who-When and Why articles were: *What Makes Popcorn Pop? Where The Turkey Got It's Name* and *What Good Are Worms?*

"I have written a great deal in the adult field, but my first love is writing for children. Writing for children requires just as much professionalism and skill as writing for adults — if not more. Children's minds are curious, interested, flexible and responsive. My goal is to write books that are so absorbing, exciting and meaningful that the reader will fall in love with them and will want to read more."

Ethel continues to swing back and forth between the adult and juvenile field. Her article, *Christmas At Uncle Dyke's Farm,* Good Old Days magazine, 1981, is a true story based on a childhood memory. Her article, *Ten Gallon Hat,* World of Rodeo and Western Heritage, 1981, is a story about Sam Houston's Hat. Another article about Paul Revere was published in Parade, 1980.

Ethel and her husband moved to Tomball, Texas in 1975 and enjoy country living. She commutes to Houston once a month to attend the meeting of the Associated Authors of Children's Literature, Houston, and is involved in several writing projects.

"Sometimes I get a little frustrated because I can't write as much as I would like too. I stay busy tending my garden and do enjoy visits from my children. But when I get involved in a writing project I usually don't have any trouble sticking with it until it's finished.

"One of my current projects is a book for boys. It is about boys, football and dogs. I can hardly wait to get back to this project.

"Writing is a hard and lonely business — but there's nothing more satisfying than to write and to sell what I write. Writing is a big, wonderful part of my life — I'm grateful for the constant challenge writing gives me."

In the brochure from Larksdale Press promoting Ethel's book, *Stowaway To Texas,* it states that, "anyone, regardless of age, will appreciate Mrs. Evey's polished writing skills and extensive research."

Ethel Lindamood Evey is another Texas writer who is constantly reaching further and doing more.

Lucy H. Wallace

15

Lucy H. Wallace

(Lucy Hopson Wallace McClelland)

"People are my prime interest: to read about or to write about. In writing for the newspaper, I have the innate feeling that everyone, no matter his station in life, has a story to tell."

Lucy Wallace is a fourth generation Texan whose career as a writer-photographer has always been firmly focused on her native state, and especially the region in and around "The Valley," the place she calls home.

Wanting to preserve some of the vast history of her region, Lucy was one of "the prime movers" in an effort to write, publish and distribute a triology — *Gift Of The Rio*, 1975, *Roots By The River*, 1978 and *Rio Grande Roundup*, 1980. All of these books were published by the Border Kingdom Press which is the publishing wing of the Valley By-Liners.

"The Valley By-Liners was organized in 1943 and was an off-shoot from the Corpus Chrisit By-Liners. Dee Woods who was from Corpus came to help us get organized. From the beginning, as now, we hold very high standards for our membership. Our membership is by invitation only and each member must be published and working as a professional writer."

After the Valley By-Liners were well established, they held Writer's Day Conferences and contributed to many public service functions. They had been wanting to tackle an in-depth writing project, one that would be of public service and would preserve the history of their region, when the Mission, Texas Bicentennial Committee commissioned them to write a book of valley history, as a contribution to the bicentennial celebration. They were delighted with the project and began to gather material and soon twenty-six writers and three artists went to work on their first book, *Gift Of The Rio.*

"This book was an anthology of history, folklore, poems and pictures."

This first book was so successful that the Valley By-Liners decided to write and produce a second book, *Roots By The River.*

"This book is about the sturdy folks who tamed the lower Rio Grande frontier. Because of their courage and their dreams for a better way of life, they left a legacy which bore fruit many years later.

"Now there is large scale irrigation, a seaside resort at Padre Island, successful flood control, water conservation and growth of the citrus industry."

Roots By The River won first place in the annual competition sponsored by the Texas Historical Commission.

In 1980, the Valley By-Liners published their third and final book, *Rio Grande Round-Up.*

"The stories in this book symbolize the diverse elements entwined in the bicultural-bilingual area known as the lower Rio Grande Valley of Texas."

Lucy describes herself as, "a late bloomer," in the writing profession.

"When I was growing up, I didn't know or even feel led toward writing as a career. I did work on the high school newspaper, but it was years before I tackled another writing project."

Lucy graduated from high school in Hubbard, Texas in 1917 and since she was only fifteen years old, her parents insisted that she stay home for a year before going to college.

When she was sixteen she stayed with relatives in Corpus Christi while she went to school for teacher training and later she taught school in several rural areas. At times, some of her students were older than she was.

"The most fun I ever had teaching was when I lived and worked on the JA Ranch which spans Palo Duro Canyon in West Texas. My students, all eight of them, were from families who worked on the ranch. Most of them rode horseback to school as I did.

"When I was young and single I had a "wanderlust nature." I taught school in a different place each year. This was the best way I knew to get out and see the country. I loved it!"

When Lucy met and married Richard Wallace in 1922, her wandering days came to an end. For the next few years she was a devoted wife and mother. During the early years of their marriage, Lucy and her husband lived in Lubbock, Edinburg and Houston. When her children began school in Houston, Lucy became active in the PTA.

While working with this organization, her leadership ability and her vision led her into many new programs. She initiated the Summer Round-Up, checking pre-schooler's health records and immunizations.

When the family moved to Harlingen, Texas, Lucy became involved with the PTA, there. It was this involvement that led her into public life and plunged her into a new career.

While doing public relations work for the PTA, Lucy met Minnie Gilbert, who was Women's Editor of the *Valley Morning Star*. When Lucy moved to Mission, Texas, Minnie Gilbert asked her if she would like to work as a stringer for *The Star*.

Lucy accepted the job and started sending handwritten copy to *The Star*. She became good at this job and was hired as stringer for the *McAllen Monitor* and *The Brownsville Herald*.

Knowing that she wanted to pursue a career in the newspaper field, Lucy bought a typewriter and began branching out into hard news and feature stories.

"My first feature story was about the little mission, La Lomita (little hill in Spanish). This is the little chapel which Mission, Texas is named for."

When the *Mission Times* acquired the daily paper where Lucy was working the editor offered Lucy a full time job with *The Times*. Lucy was quick to accept this new challenge and worked as Women's Editor and eventually progressed to News

Editor and Photographer. She worked full time for this newspaper for 20 years.

Joe T. Cook, Editor of *The Times*, said that Lucy was the best asset *The Times* acquired when they took over the other paper.

"When I was working as News Editor, I was on call 24 hours a day, but this really wasn't too bad because I was a widow —my husband died in 1940, and I needed to be totally involved at that time. It was my job to see that the news was covered, regardless of the hour it happened.

"Around 1944, I decided to buy a big press camera and learn to use it. Then I would be able to take the pictures as well as write the story."

Because of her job as News Editor and Photographer, Lucy was able to meet, photograph and write about most of the dignitaries who came to Mission and the surrounding area.

When President Dwight Eisenhower met the President of Mexico for the dedication of the Falcon Dam, which is about 100 miles from Mission, Lucy was on the job covering the story for *The Times*.

"President Eisenhower was a guest of Allan Shivers who was the Governor of Texas at that time. The Shivers' valley home was the "Little White House". Of course, the press from all across the country was swarming all over Mission. There were lots of press parties and a bus to transport the press to the dam.

"I was able to get two good pictures of the President at the ceremony and one of him and Governor Shivers the next day at church. It was lucky for me that Governor Shivers brought the President to my church and of course, I always had my camera nearby and snapped a good picture as they were walking out of the building."

As a news photographer, Lucy photographed other dignitaries including two Mexican Presidents and several Texas Governors; Beauford Jester, Price Daniel and Dolph Briscoe; and four governors of Mexican states.

In 1950, Lucy's article, *Governor In The Cabbage Patch*, was the cover story for Texas magazine, the Sunday supplement of the *Houston Chronicle* newspaper.

"This was an article about Governor Shivers' visit to the Valley. I photographed him in the cabbage patch because I wanted to show his tie-in with the Valley."

Lucy sold another article to the *Houston Chronicle* written about a hometown boy, Lloyd Bentsen.

"This is Lloyd Bentsen's hometown and I have been writing about him ever since he entered public life. He was county judge in Hidalgo county when he was a very young man. The article I sold to the *Chronicle* was written when he was judge.

"He moved up to Representative and later Senator. I took lots of pictures of him during his campaign for President."

During her twenty years with the *Mission Times*, Lucy received many awards from the Texas Press Women and the National Federation of Press Women for special editions, news editing, feature stories and photography.

From 1966 to 1976, Lucy worked as editor for the Rio Grande Valley Yearbook.

"This is a valley and northern Mexico regional annual periodical. The man who owned the publication handled the advertising and I wrote the editorials and furnished the pictures.

"The Yearbook stayed on the newstand for one year, then we put out a new one. It was my job to report on each town's progress and I tried to include something about every town in the valley."

Lucy was always broadening her involvement in the publishing world and during World War II, she was editor of *The Sunbath Dispatch*, a publication of Moore Air Base. This job went hand in hand with her Red Cross work.

"I was the Red Cross Representative in Mission and helped contact servicemen's families. During this time I wrote many, many articles relating to local servicemen and conducted interviews for UPI."

In 1965, after being a widow for nearly 25 years, Lucy married Charles F. McClelland, who encouraged and assisted her in the publication of her book, *The Incredible City*. Before his death in 1979, they traveled extensively in the western part of the United States, Mexico and Europe. While Lucy gathered material for articles and books, Charlie was an avid rock-hound.

"I met Charlie on my first trip to Real de Catorce, Mexico. I had met a woman who lived near this town and became intrigued with the city. I was determined to make a trip there. I went with the idea of writing an article and took lots of pictures.

"Charlie and I had mutual friends and met through them. He was a retired builder from Tacoma, Washington and came here to spend the winters.

"Charlie was the one who encouraged me to write the book. He felt there was too much material for an article. He told me that if I would write the book he would publish it.

"I started the project and before it was finished we decided to get married. I guess you could say that this book was indirectly responsible for us getting together."

The book, *The Incredible City,* Amigo Enterprises, is the story of Real de Catorce, San Luis Potosi state, Mexico — an old mining town built in the 1770's.

"The book is really a pictorial essay. I made so many trips there that I lost track. I took most of the pictures which are in the book except the very old ones. I was very fortunate because this place had been founded by a very wealthy family who lived very well while the city was in it's heyday.

"These old pictures were just fabulous because they reflect the wealth and lifestyle of those people."

The book is in it's second printing and is still in demand. Since this is the only English language book about Real de Catorce, the Mexican tourist bureaus have expressed appreciation to Lucy for her book and the interest it has generated in Real de Catorce as a tourist attraction.

The book won first place in the state and national competition sponsored by the Press Women in 1965.

In 1977, Lucy worked with the Cleo Dawson Foundation and was instrumental in getting Dr. Cleo Dawson's book, *She Came To The Valley,* a story about pioneer Mission, brought back into print.

When the movie, *She Came To The Valley,* was released in 1980 by RGV Pictures, Lucy handled all of the local publicity. She was busy taking pictures of Sissy Spacek, Colonel Harlan

Sanders and Freddie Fender. She also had a bit part in the movie.

"People have always been my prime interest: to read about or to write about. In writing for the newspaper, I have the innate feeling that everyone, no matter his station in life, has a story to tell.

"For a weekly paper, close to the people, it was my mission to find that story in the little man. The story I am writing may be the only time that the blacksmith or the woman in the quilting club, will ever have their name in print.

"I like to dig out these stories and spotlight the common man as much as possible. I was once cited by my fellow staffers for the length of the obituaries I wrote."

Lucy believes that if an aspiring writer will follow the advice given by Mark Twain many years ago, they will succeed in the writing field or will at least give it a fighting chance.

"Mark Twain had the right idea. When friends or relatives asked his advice about how to go about getting employment, he told them something to this effect: pick the type of work you want most, then the place of employment. Go to the boss and offer to work two weeks or a month for free to prove to him that you can make good for him and yourself.

"If you really feel qualified and you really want that job, your offer will start you on a career. This is good advice.

"I believe that the experience of working on a weekly newspaper is the best training for a young person bent on a journalistic career. Whether it follows or proceeds formal journalism courses in college. This type of work offers two precious ingredients for any writing career — discipline and challenge."

"I haven't had many real disappointments in my writing career. I've had a few things turned down, but not many. I know my markets and I try to write material that will sell to them. It's important to know your market. It saves a great deal of time and many disappointments."

Lucy says that when she joins a group she always gets stuck with handling the publicity. But there are some special projects that she enjoys working with and spends a great deal of time promoting.

One of these projects is Archives Alert, a group that is collecting photographs and documents to be photographed and preserved for future generations.

Lucy is also actively promoting and assisting in the preparation of a history of Hidalgo County as part of the celebration of the sesquicentennial of Texas in 1986. Much of her vast and comprehensive collection of data, old newspapers and photographs will be included in this history.

She is also working on a project with several other writers spotlighting 100 women who have made their mark or have contributed to the progress of the valley area.

Whether writing newspaper feature stories of the unsung person in the community or writing and photographing the famous, Lucy's professionalism and skill are always evident.

"I'm sold on my part of the world and I am content to be a regional writer — a newspaper woman. This is what I know — and love."

Lucy will be remembered for her dedication and hard work as one of the "grassroots historians." Doing just a little bit more (Poquita Más) to preserve the treasured history of her region and reaching across the border to share her talents with her friends and neighbors there.

16

Beatrice S. Levin

"All of my work is obliquely autobiographical — it stems from something that interested me — fascinated me or happened to me."

After a person has been working in the marketplace for forty years, he is usually looking forward to the time when he can retire. He may be dreaming of living in a retirement village in Florida, where life is less hectic or he may simply want to have more time to pursue a hobby or to travel. For whatever reason, most people feel that forty years of work is a big enough chunk out of their life.

There are exceptions, of course. One of these exceptions is the professional writer. Usually the writer is not thinking of retirement, but is eagerly awaiting the next stage in his life — depending on his experiences to furnish him with fresh new ideas for a book, a poem, a song, an article or a short story.

This has been true in the life of Beatrice Levin. She has been writing — and writing everyday — for the past forty years.

"Frankly, I don't know how people survive if they don't have the therapy of writing or composing or painting. The world has so much melancholy.

"There is a little poem by Dorothy Parker which goes something like: a mother, wife or authoress — thank God I'm content with less.

"I've never been content with less. Some of the things I have done have not been anything more than personal essays or

Beatrice S. Levin

observations about what was going on in my life at the time, but there has always been some editor who was consistently accepting my work.

"My success may be small potatoes compared to some, but for the past forty years, there hasn't been a year when I haven't had an income from my writing. I have written everyday. My son, Philip, complains. He says, 'Mama, nobody works everyday. People take weekends off.'

"It's just second nature for me to go to my desk when I'm home and when I'm not at home, I'm still thinking about writing. Whatever I'm doing is grist for the mill."

When Beatrice was a very young child, living in Providence, Rhode Island, she was busy writing stories. Her mother gave her long laundry lists and she scribbled her stories on the back of them.

By the time she was in junior high school, she was publishing in the student section of Scholastic magazine. While she was attending Central High School, she edited the school yearbook and was editor-writer for the literary magazine, Crest.

When she entered Rhode Island College in Providence, she knew she wanted to be a writer, but she took a realistic approach in her degree program.

"I knew I needed a way to support myself, so I took a teaching degree — wanting to specialize in teaching the gifted — and teaching English. But I still had a great interest in writing and edited the college newspaper, *The Anchor*, and wrote for the literary magazine."

Even though she took a realistic approach to her degree program and attained a Bachelor of Education Degree in 1942, writing was still high on her list of priorities and after she graduated she went to New York City and took a job with *Woman's Day* magazine.

"I worked in the neighbors section, sorting and editing the letters from the readers. The best letters were paid for and published in the magazine. I worked for Woman's Day about a year and then went to work setting up an index for Encyclopedia Americana."

Because of her outstanding work while employed by Encyclopedia Americana, setting up an extensive index, Beatrice was offered an unusual opportunity to participate in a new branch of the Women's Army Corps.

"In 1943, the army asked me to join the WAC and do editorial work for them. After my training, I landed at Camp Wolters, Texas, with a teaching unit."

While at Camp Wolters, Beatrice wrote for the *Camp Wolter's Longhorn* paper and was later transferred into public relations. She wrote scripts for a radio show and handled an orientation program.

While she was completing her two year stint in the Army, she heard about a play writing contest which offered a fellowship to the University of Wisconsin Drama Department for the best play written by a soldier. She wrote a play, *Until This Day,* submitted it to the contest and won the fellowship.

After she got out of the service, she went to Wisconsin to claim her fellowship.

"My father didn't want me to go to the University and said if I didn't go he would buy me a fur coat. I really didn't want a fur coat, but I was so angry with my father that I went down and bought myself a fur coat on the installment plan.

"My father came to the United States from Romania right after his barmitzvah. He was just thirteen years old and had to go right to work and he didn't have any more formal education.

"I was sort of the sport in the family. I was the first girl, on either side, to go to college. It was a special favor to let a girl go through high school. There was some encouragement for the boys to get a higher education because they were expected to earn the living, but there was a good deal of opposition against women.

"My father and I really didn't get along very well because he found me threatening — in my intellectual and creative pursuits."

Indirectly, the fur coat which Beatrice bought with a $25.00 down payment was responsible for her meeting her future husband, Franklyn Levin.

"I met my husband the first day I was on campus. He was also starting his doctorate. He was standing behind me in a line and I asked him if he would hold my place in the line while I hung up my installment plan fur coat.

"He agreed and when I came back he told me that since there wasn't anyone in the locker room to watch the coat there was a good chance it would be stolen. Then he began lecturing me about the falacies of buying on the installment plan — which goes on even now after 35 years.

"He bought my lunch that day and I was charmed by him. He had a fantastic sense of humor. He was full of jokes. We really went for each other very fast. I guess we were both ready. I was 26 and he was a little younger, but it's worked out fine."

After they were married they stayed in Madison, Wisconsin, and attended the university working on their doctorates. When Frank was hired by Carter Oil Company which was a subsidiary of Exxon, they moved to Tulsa, Oklahoma.

Beatrice became a book reviewer for the Tulsa World and started circulating a book, *The Lonely Room,* which she had written as a graduate student.

"I was in Mari Sandoz's creative writing class and she was extremely encouraging. After the book was finished I decided on Bobbs-Merrill as a publisher because they were in the same city where my husband's family lived. I took the book to them and one of the editors, Rosemary York, called a few days later and said that she really loved the book, but it needed a lot of work. She wanted to know if I would be willing to do the work. I said, 'sure!'

"She taught me something that I think other writers might benefit from. She said it was important for the reader to be aware of how much time is passing. The characters need to be in a specific place — a specific room or a specific city. I learned to anchor my characters in a specific setting instead of having them flying around in space.

"I rewrote that book three times before I got it right. When they finally accepted it I received a telegram from Rosemary York which read, the third time is the charm."

The book, *The Lonely Room,* was published in 1950 and was a best seller in many cities.

"The story was about a girl growing up in Rhode Island,

falling in love with an unsuitable young man and going into service for two years.

"It was loosely autobiographical — all of my work is obliquely autobiographical — it stems from something that interested me — fascinated me or happened to me.

"Needless to say, I was enormously excited when the book hit the marketplace. This was my first novel. It had not been written under ideal conditions in some respects, but it wasn't that bad either.

"Frank and I were both in college. This was very, very unusual in those days. Usually a woman dropped out when she married and the husband's lifestyle dictated the family lifestyle.

"Frank and I were different. We took turns going to school, tending the baby and keeping the house in order. Of course, I did a lot of things for him, but I didn't give up my life. If there were sacrifices, they went both ways, but we never looked at it as sacrifices. This was just our way of life."

The publication of this first book gave Beatrice the encouragement she needed to tackle other book projects. None of her work ever fell into a neat stereotyped writing form. It was as varied as the colors in a rainbow.

The Singer And The Summer Song, Acardia House, 1964, paperback, Berkley, 1974; is a teen-age love story. *Safari Smith, Peace Corps Nurse,* Universal Press, 1965; *Women In Medicine,* Scarecrow Press, 1979; *Eyewitness to Exodus,* Universal Press, 1963; and *John Hawk, White Man, Black Man, Indian Chief,* May Davenport, 1982.

She also wrote four books for American Indian children for the Montana Program for Indians and published a collection of short stories, *Hidden Treasures,* Larksdale, 1980.

"I enjoyed writing the books for the Indian children. We lived in Oklahoma for fifteen years and I was absolutely fascinated by the Osage and Seminole Indians. When I read an article in one of the trade magazines expressing a need for books written for the Indian children who were poor or reluctant readers, I just couldn't pass up the opportunity to write for them.

"The editor made copies of the stories and sent them to various schools to have the Indian children illustrate them. I thought this was a charming idea. The best drawings were included in the books and the children were paid for their work. This was an added bonus for them.''

While Beatrice was working on these books, she became even more interested in the Seminoles and wrote, *John Hawk, White Man, Black Man, Indian Chief.*

''This story is about a slave who lived in Georgia and ran away to Florida to join the Seminole Indians. This was a very common practice. The Seminoles took the runaways in and because of their knowledge about farming they were usually regarded as special and became chiefs.

''I worked on this book for seven years. The first year was devoted to research. I made a trip to Mexico to research the Mexican War. Everything I turned up on John Hawk looked like myths, legends or half-truths, so I decided to write the story as fiction.''

Once Beatrice has written a book or short story, she usually sticks with the work until it is published, no matter how long it takes. She kept one of her stories, *Ghost From An Enchanter Fleeing,* circulating for six years before it was accepted by Ball State Forum, a magazine of Ball State University in Muncie, Indiana. The story was later picked up by Best American Short Stories and was listed among the most distinguished short stories in 1972.

''This story came out of my experiences teaching on a black college campus. The story is loosely based on one of Shelley's poems which says; oh west wind — thou, from whose unseen presence the leaves dead are driven, like ghosts from an enchanter fleeing, yellow, and black, and pale, and hectic red. Pestilence — stricken multitudes.

''As I stated in the story, the lines had a new meaning for me — the ''pestilence — stricken multitudes, yellow and black, and pale — .'' That's us — all of us, driven by winds, both destroyer and preserver.''

Beatrice has reached the point where she does not get as upset when a manuscript comes back. There were times when she was so depressed about her writing that her husband wanted her to give it up. "Give it up," he said. "There are so many other things you can do successfully."

When she was working on the book, *Eyewitness To Exodus*, she did extensive research with microfilm and studied every single piece of information she could find. She wanted her characters to be real people, taken from real life. She did not believe in characters who were myths or legends or seven feet tall.

"I believe every character must have an ample human view of things — sometimes my characters are ugly or inconsistent. This is the way real people are. I always strive to give my characters human traits.

I worked on this book for a very long time and finally sold it to Reconstruction Press. They held the manuscript for four years. In the meantime, Leon Uris's book, *Exodus*, was published and became a best seller.

"The editor from Reconstruction Press returned my manuscript with the comment that my idea must have come from Leon Uris's book, even though this editor had the manuscript in his possession several years before Leon's book came out.

"This was a great disappointment to me. It set me back for months. I can remember going shopping, trying to get my mind off the book, but it didn't help much.

"I was very upset when I was heading back to my car and wasn't paying any attention to the traffic light and stepped out into the street against the light. A policeman called me down and gave me a walking ticket.

"I've learned to cope much better now. When something comes back, I know it's not the end of the world. I just bundle it up and ship it off again."

Over the past forty years, Beatrice has sold over four hundred short stories and articles and has published twelve books.

The subjects for her articles and short stories have been as varied as her books.

Some of her articles include; *Campus Negroes and Anti-Semitism*, Hadassah; *Thimbleful Of Youth*, an article about the Oklahoma youth orchestra, Oklahoma Orbit; *Horses In Art*, Hoofs and Horns; *Leisure And The Cuckoo Clock*, The Villager; *When Your Child Has A Speech Problem*, Rosary; *Ancient Art*

Of Stained Glass Windows, Christian Science Monitor; *Say O.K. When You're Offered Okra,* Tulsa World; *Winning The Wives,* Industrial Research; *What Is Your Adolescent Reading Tonight?* Denver Post; and a three part series, *So You Want To Write,* Christian Science Monitor.

Just a few of her many short stories include: *Old Man On A Park Bench,* Church and Home; *State of Grace,* Catholic Home; *Paris Is A City Of Love,* The Villager; *The House That Jack Would Build,* Teens; *The Dummy,* University of Kansas City Review and *Uproar In The Rye,* Cordette.

While she was working in public relations for the Junior Chamber of Commerce, she wrote several booklets to help raise social consciousness; *Mental Health and Mental Retardation, Raising Funds For Charity* and *Parks and Playgrounds For Your Community.*

Changing hats again, Beatrice was public relations coordinator and writer for the Sterling International Travel Corporation. She enjoys writing travel articles and has been published in the International Travel News and other fine travel magazines.

Besides her interest in travel, Beatrice is very interested in the field of health and medicine. Her articles have appeared in Practicing Physician, Healthways and Health magazines.

With the constant demands for articles, stories, book reviews and her many book projects, some requiring many months and sometimes years of research, it would seem almost impossible for Beatrice to pursue a second career. But she does — she has been teaching creative writing for the Spring Branch School District, adult division, for the past eighteen years.

She has also been a scholar and teacher at some very outstanding institutions around the world. She took part in a teacher-exchange program sponsored by the University of Jerusalem. She was a scholar at the Shakespeare Institute, Stratford-upon-Avon, England; University of Hawaii; Bread Loaf Writer's Conference; Black Studies Program; Professional Playwright's Seminar and Hill College, Abergavenny, Wales.

She has been a scholar or teacher in special programs at more than 20 major universities around the world.

"I enjoy traveling and consider myself to be a child of the

universe. I get homesick for places I've never been.''

To the aspiring writer, Beatrice says, ''A writer is like a fine seamstress who has made a beautiful patchwork quilt. When it is finished it is a true work of art. She can tell where every little piece of material originated. She may say, this was an old wedding dress — this was a silk scarf my grandmother gave me.

''This is the way a story emerges. It's truth, but it still emerges through the imagination of the writer.''

Even though Beatrice has had a long successful career in the writing field, she feels that her most successful achievements have been in the classroom.

''Teaching is a very big part of my life. I try to be as encouraging as I can to my students. If they want to write novels, I tell them to write novels, but write other things that will sell quickly, while the novel is working.

''Write out of your own experiences — do book reviews — articles on having a party. I have had hundreds of articles published about my children — about my experiences with moving — traveling — entertaining.

''Write about whatever is happening to you. These are the articles that will sell quickly.

''Recently my husband and I talked about building a beach house — again. I've wanted a beach house all of my life, so for the past 30 years I've been collecting little items about beach houses and tucking them away in a folder, hoping that someday this will no longer be a dream, but a reality.

''I was looking through the file and realized that I had enough material for a good article. I wrote, *My Dream House,* and sold it to the Christian Science Monitor. This may be as far as it ever gets, but I did put the little items which I had collected to good use.

''This is one of the special joys of writing — writing about what you know, what you love and what you are interested in.''

Even after forty years, teaching and working as a writer, Beatrice continues to travel fulfilling her teaching responsibilities and storing up information for her writing projects.

Each summer she travels to a small college near Shrewsbury, Wales and teaches a six weeks creative writing class.

"I have been teaching this class for the past four summers. I love it, but I find myself fighting fatigue when I travel on a work-holiday and plan to steal a year and just take a leisurely vacation next year.

"My husband and I had a fantastic month in France, with a week on the Riviera. I managed to lock us out on a balcony of a plush hotel. The door locked automatically — and we had quite an adventure getting sprung."

If Beatrice runs true to form, this trip and this adventure will show up in one of her short stories or articles.

Juanita Bourns

17

Juanita Bourns

"I have always felt that I had a calling to write. Sometimes I have such an urgency — such an inner compulsion to get my poems written down — I just must do it."

In the February 1982 issue of the Pacifica Nexus magazine there is one full page devoted to Juanita Bourns' poetry. One poem in the magazine defines her view of the illusive, yet compelling form of writing which we call poetry.

> Profusion of images does not
> necessarily constitute disunity.
> As pebbles grow from stone, so
> particulars grow from universals,
> where undercurrents of the ages
> swirl into waters of now.
> Wonder of stars —
> that space contains
> all there is of time.

"What I deal with in writing my poetry is the feeling, the idea and the picture images. I try to work toward fitting the proper words to the feeling — the idea — and the picture images."

Juanita believes that it is important for a poem to reach more than one level in order for the poem to be successful. She has always been strongly influenced by her environment and many of her poems have come out of her own experiences.

"When I was very young my mother read nursery rhymes to me and I was always delighted when I could repeat some of the nonsense words. I liked to hear the rhythm."

Juanita wrote her first poem when she was in the fourth grade. It was about the peach tree that graced their backyard. Even then she felt the urgency to write poetry.

Juanita was born in Weir, Texas, but her family moved to Oklahoma when she was very young.

"We moved to Westville, Oklahoma when I was about seven. My father bought a rocky farm—one that was impossible for him to farm, so after about a year we moved to Port, Oklahoma, where I grew up. I grew up on a farm during the depression years.

"My parents had a great influence on me because my father always wanted us to do our very best in school. My mother had attended Baylor University and liked just a little bit getting a degree in liberal arts. She did get a teacher's certificate and taught school for several years. She had written some poetry and always enjoyed reading to us.

"One of my uncles, Roy Storrs, wrote poetry. We had some great talks together.

"When I was in high school, my teachers were enthusiastic about my poetry, but I was a bit self-conscious about it. People seem to either look down on or up to anyone who is different enough to write poetry."

From the beginning, Juanita's poetry has reflected her love for nature and has been indicative of her lifestyle.

She grew up in the midst of beautiful cottonwood and elm trees and played along the banks of a rambling creek which crossed their farm. She walked among the many wildflowers that grew in the pastures in the springtime and tramped through the icy snow to milk the cows in the winter.

These experiences were her inspiration when she wrote: *Walk In The Woods; A Ride In Snow; In The Cotton Seed Bin; Blue Daisies Grow By The Windmill* and *Farm Wife*.

After Juanita graduated from Port High School as valedictorian, she entered Southwestern State College and attained a Bachelor of Arts Degree.

She met and married her husband, Charles Bourns, at Southwestern and they were married May 20, 1939.

After Charles graduated from college his work took them over much of the United States, Latin America and Hawaii. Juanita taught high school English, creative writing and journalism in Oklahoma, Texas, Utah, Nevada, California and Hawaii.

During World War II, Charles served as a naval officer and Juanita followed him as much as possible. When he was stationed in Pensacola, Florida, she took her two young daughters and moved there to be with Charles.

"Since I grew up in the inlands, I was unacquainted with the abundance of water that surrounded Pensacola. I was absolutely fascinated by the translucence of the waves and thought it was marvelous to see how the fish would swim up inside of the waves. I kept this image in my mind for a very long time and finally wrote a poem to express my feelings and called it, *White Caps*.

"These aqua waves are fringed with frothy lace/ Like ruffles on a sea-green velvet gown;/ I gasp for breath to feel them splash my face — ."

This was Juanita's first published poem. It was published in the Texas Outlook magazine.

Another poem, *Wind Song*, was also inspired by nature.

"I was on my way home from work one afternoon and I could feel the briskly cool gulf wind against my face. This felt so exciting and sort of put me on a high. I could hardly wait to get home in order to write down the words to express this feeling."

A dream hounded Juanita until it took shape and became a poem which she called, *Arrival*. This poem was published in the July 1975 issue of The Writer magazine.

"I dreamed that my husband and I were on a train. The only other couple on the train was a very old man and woman. The old woman was aware of a turbulent storm outside and tried to get her sleeping husband to wake up to see the storm."

> John, we're alone
> this train striking thunder
> under its wheels
> rain from its windows

and thunder cracks
that ghost ship
in the clouds
brave against blue lightning.

John, wake up to me.
That ghost ship holds
spilling into wind
our Johnny, our Ann.

and you
in your Captain's hat
asleep. John, the train
has stopped.

Juanita believes this poem is a plea to be understood.

Three other poems published in The Writer were: *Tamers,* July, 1973, *Farm Wife,* September, 1974, and *The Teacher,* July, 1979.

One of the biggest thrills for Juanita was getting her poem, *Creative Student,* published in the May 1974 issue of the Spring Poetry Festival of the English Journal. This is the journal of the National Association of Teachers of English.

"This idea came when I was teaching high school English in Kailua, Hawaii. One of my students was a very artistic person. He would come to class some days and say, 'Mrs. Bourns, what are we going to do today?' After I would tell him, he would say, 'I don't want to do that. I feel like being creative.' I would say, okay, be creative and then you can do the class work later.

"He was a real joy. He might write a short story or a poem and then illustrate it."

While others
dip spoons
into potliquor

Garry ladles
essence of galaxies
into his bowl.

They gallop stick horses
through puddles
of ifs and buts

while he on a bubble
ties wings to rainbow
fish, cloud-caught

nets them in language
drops them before me
throbbing on the grass.

In 1949, when they were in Las Cruces, New Mexico, Juanita worked for radio station KOBE. She was "keeper of the log" and did some script writing.

"I wrote introductions for some of the musical selections. They were usually short, but I enjoyed the work."

There were times when Juanita didn't do anything except housework and tend the children, which was not all she wanted to be doing. When she got a chance to work at something really creative, such as teaching or working for the radio station she was delighted.

"I always looked for creative jobs and was usually lucky enough to find them."

When she lived in New Mexico, she attended some classes at A&M University and had a poem, *Lilac Time,* published in the college anthology.

"During our married life, Charles and I moved around a great deal because of his work. At times I was reluctant to move, but when he was sent to Sao Paolo, Brazil, I was thrilled and really wanted to go.

"But the trip turned out to be quite different from what I expected. Living conditions were terrible. Charles was working as an Engineer for Nelson Rockefeller's company, The International Basic Economy Corporation. His job was to help improve the rural life in Brazil by building roads, saw mills and making many other improvements.

"Sometimes he would be working in the interior for three weeks at a time. This left me alone in a strange country to care for the children.

"I decided it would be best for me and the children to come home."

Juanita did not let this experience go to waste. She wrote several poems expressing her feelings about life in Brazil.

At Butantan Snake Farm, The Christ Of Corcovado and *To Say Goodbye*. All of these poems were later included in the book, *Inward A Jungle*.

THE CHRIST OF CORCOVADO

That cross
Fire in this tropic night
Is it fear bumps my heart
       stops it
           in my throat

I seem to recall
was it promise or threat
that out from ultimate grief
comes reckoning. Ultimate.

When Juanita was living in Pacifica, California, she was sending her poems out regularly, but she wasn't selling any of them. She knew she needed some professional advice about her work, so she enrolled in a creative writing class at Skyline College and started studying under Rich Yurman.

"While I was in this class, Rich helped me get about one hundred poems in publishable form. Enough for the book, *Inward A Jungle*.

"When I lived in San Francisco, I took some courses at the San Francisco State University and my professor, Michael Wild, really gave me the inspiration I needed to write most of the poems for the book.

"One of the best things that happened to me at Skyline College was meeting Erni Scocca. Erni said, 'Juanita, when we get together poetry happens.'

"Our professor, Rich Yurman said, 'Juanita, when you and Erni get together, the cross pollination is marvelous.'

In the dedication page of the book, *Inward A Jungle*, Juanita gives both of these men full credit for their influence in her life and work.

She says, ''To Michael Wild — who woke the dream and set it moving. To Rich Yurman — who with insight and sensitivity helped me bring it to life.''

Both Juanita and her husband were native Texans and in 1979 after Charles retired, they decided to move back to Texas. They settled in Houston to be near one of their daughters, Marquita Macon and her family.

''Marquita is an artist and after Charles retired he wanted to come to Houston and perhaps establish an art gallery.''

But as sometimes happens, plans can change over night. They had already bought a house and moved their furniture in when they found out that Marquita's husband's company had transferred him to New Orleans, Louisiana.

Tragedy seemed to stalk Juanita for the next two years. Her mother died and close on the heels of this death, Charles was struck down by a sudden and fatal heart attack.

''After Charles died, this left me alone in Houston, except for one brother, but I decided to stay in Houston and start rebuilding my life — alone.''

Needing an outlet for her time and her talent, Juanita joined the Houston Poetry Society and became very active. She began entering some of her poems in local and state contests and took many first place awards.

Some of the poems to win first place were: *Physician; Dream Of The Faun; Eulogy For Charles; Siren* and *Passage.*

She won two first place awards in the Texas annual contest sponsored by the Texas State Poetry Society with her poems: *Your Cabin Crumbled* and *To Beyond Beginning.*

Juanita says that if you really want to be a poet, the first thing you must do is write.

''Get something down on paper — then if you don't know what to do with it, go to someone who does and get help.

''I have always felt that I had a calling to write. Sometimes I have such an urgency — such an inner compulsion to get my poems written down — I just must do it.''

Juanita is busy working on a new crop of poems to be published in a second book—a book of love poems dedicated to the memory of her husband, Charles.

As always, her poetry gives her new courage and a freshness for life.

Just a sample of the beauty and challenge to be found in her new book include: *Contingency* and *Illusion*.

CONTINGENCY

How can I paint
      this sunrise —
tint the morning sky
when storm clouds
      overcast your eyes?
My brush goes stiff
      and dry.

If I must paint
      a sunset
or fling a rainbow
      high,
first
      let me stop
        that rivulet
before it leaves
      your eye.

ILLUSION

I hear blue jay squawk
See squirrel's tail flick
Beyond blue space that dips
into pine, I see you walk
down-sky
      in khaki pants
in broad-brim hat.

You squint through your lens
See squawk of the jay
See squirrel's tail flick
See wind-strummed
sway of the pine.

You click the shutter
      Then
out from the sun
you return to the sun

And I am alone again.